Pearls *of* Wisdom

ALSO BY BARBARA BUSH

Pearls of Wisdom

LITTLE PIECES OF ADVICE
(THAT GO A LONG WAY)

Barbara Bush

TWELVE

New York Boston

Twelve
Hachette Book Group
1290 Avenue of the Americas, New York, NY 10104
twelvebooks.com
twitter.com/twelvebooks

First Edition: March 2020

Twelve is an imprint of Grand Central Publishing. The Twelve name and logo are trademarks of Hachette Book Group, Inc.

The publisher is not responsible for websites (or their content) that are not owned by the publisher.

The Hachette Speakers Bureau provides a wide range of authors for speaking events. To find out more, go to www.hachettespeakersbureau.com or call (866) 376-6591.

The excerpt from "For Mrs. Bush," published in the *New York Times* on April 20, 2018, is used with permission of the author, James McBride.

The excerpt from "We can all learn from Barbara Bush's life lessons to these Maine third-graders," published in the *Bangor Daily News* on May 3, 2018, is used with permission of the author, Cherrie MacInnes, and the *Bangor Daily News*.

The op-ed piece "Barbara Bush visited our facility for children with HIV/AIDS. It was unforgettable," published in the *Washington Post* on April 21, 2018, is used with permission of the authors, Debbie Tate and Joan McCarley, and the *Washington Post*.

The excerpt from "Barbara Bush Faces Death with Courage," published in the *Wall Street Journal* on April 16, 2018, is used with permission of the author, Marc Siegel.

Library of Congress Cataloging-in-Publication Data
Names: Bush, Barbara, 1925-2018, author.
Title: Pearls of wisdom : little pieces of advice (that go a long way) / Barbara Bush.
Description: First edition. | New York : Twelve, 2020. | Summary: "The best advice First Lady Barbara Bush offered her family, staff, and close friends"–Provided by publisher.
Identifiers: LCCN 2019041814 | ISBN 9781538734940 (hardcover) | ISBN 9781538734933 (ebook)
Subjects: LCSH: Bush, Barbara, 1925-2018–Quotations. |
Presidents' spouses–United States–Quotations.
Classification: LCC E883.B87 A25 2020 | DDC 973.928092 [B]–dc23
LC record available at https://lccn.loc.gov/2019041814

ISBNs: 978-1-5387-3494-0 (hardcover), 978-1-5387-3493-3 (ebook)

Printed in the United States of America

LSC-C

10 9 8 7 6 5 4 3 2 1

Contents

Author's Note

You might question how someone who left this good earth two years ago could be the author of a new book.

Simple, really. It was her words—taken from diary entries, letters, speeches, and the memories of the people who knew and loved her—that made this book possible. It is indeed written in her voice and in her spirit.

My role was to gather the information, put it all in one place, and serve as the narrator. It was a perfect fit, since her voice is still in my ear. I worked for Barbara Bush for twenty-nine years: four years in the White House as one of her deputy press secretaries, and then in a variety of roles from 1993 until she died. I was her book editor, speechwriter, and sometimes even an adviser. (She listened to my advice at least once or twice.)

During most of those twenty-nine years, from 1994 until he died on November 30, 2018, I was also President Bush's chief of staff. Needless to say, Mrs. Bush was one of my mentors and main advisers. (I listened to her advice a lot.)

So to be her "ghostwriter" for this final book of hers was what you might call an easy lift.

There are certain things in the book of which she would not approve. "It's too much about me, Jean." We'll ignore that one.

And it is occasionally repetitious. She hated repetition in speeches and essays. So I apologize to her and to you for that flaw. My excuse: Although our contributors occasionally talk about the same "pearl," each story or example is unique or funny or dear enough, I thought you would want to see it. If nothing else, by the time you finish this book, you will get the points she was trying to make.

To help you navigate all the different voices in this book, we have used a variety of fonts:

- **Everything Mrs. Bush said is in bold.**
- Our guest contributors speak in regular font.
- *The narrator speaks in italics.*

Before we begin, a few acknowledgments:

- In addition to Mrs. Bush, this book would not have been possible without the contributions from friends and family. Your memories and stories brought Mrs. Bush back to life for all of us.

- A special thanks to the staff of the George H. W. Bush Library, without whom no book about George and Barbara Bush could ever really be written. At least not an accurate book. Head archivist Debbie Wheeler and her team were, as always, stars.
- Chase Untermeyer, who thankfully volunteered to read the galley proof.
- This book would not exist without the support and encouragement of Sean Desmond at Twelve. A special thanks to him and his team.
- And a thank-you to my two sisters, Millie Aulbur and JoAnn Heppermann, who read the early drafts and had great ideas and guidance. They hounded me about the repetition.

They also had one really good question for me, which I did not put in the book: What did I learn from Barbara Bush in thirty years?

Answer: Everything contained in these pages, but for me, **choose happiness** was her most important lesson.

I hope she knows helping her with this book—our third book project together—made me very happy.

Jean Becker

Foreword

There are those who might say Mother was bossy.

Others might call her opinionated. I was certainly on the receiving end of many strongly worded pieces of advice. Fortunately, a few of them took. As I've always said, I inherited my daddy's eyes and my mother's mouth.

Simply put, Mom could be a bit of a "blurter." And she had a wonderful sense of humor. In my last conversation with her on this earth, I called to tell her I loved her. "I love you too," she responded, "and you're my favorite son—on the phone." It was classic Barbara Bush. With trademark delivery, Mom's humor lightened the mood. She was quipping into the grave. And it put me at ease knowing that her soul was at ease.

Barbara Bush was much more than just a sharp tongue. Sure, she could be tough and intimidating. But as you'll find out in this book, her honesty came from a heart for others.

For those of us who had the great privilege of knowing and loving Mother, to keep all her great advice to ourselves would be selfish. You could say it has given us a bit of a competitive advantage in life.

The purpose of this book is to share the advice and life lessons the friends and family of Barbara Bush have been keeping in their hearts. You will hear from her children and grandchildren, extended family members, friends and former staff, presidents and prime ministers, and a celebrity or two.

We all have at least one thing in common: We adored Barbara Bush, and we are better people for having listened to her.

George W. Bush
Oldest child of Barbara Bush
43rd president of the United States

Glossary of Contributors

The family and friends of Barbara Bush are the real authors of the first two chapters of this book, as they gladly shared their "pearls of wisdom." Here are short bios of these "guest" authors. One last note: References to President Bush and to Mrs. Bush are, respectively, referencing George Herbert Walker Bush and Barbara Bush, unless otherwise noted.

CHAPTER 1

Andrews, Elizabeth (Lizzie): Daughter of Neil and Maria Bush, she is in her last year of medical school at Texas A&M College of Medicine. She lives in Houston and is engaged to Robby.

Bush, Ashley: Ashley lives in Los Angeles with her husband, Julian, where they work as TV writers. They currently have a half-hour TV show in development with Ash Atalla (producer of *The Office*) set in East Texas. Ashley also directs documentaries, most recently winning an Audience Award at the Dallas International Film Festival for *The Queen's New Clothes*.

Bush, Barbara, Sr.: First Lady of the United States from 1989 to 1993, she was born in Rye, New York, to Marvin and Pauline Pierce on June 8, 1925. She married George Herbert Walker Bush on January 6, 1945. They had six children—George W., Robin, Jeb, Neil, Marvin, and Doro. Robin died of leukemia at age three in 1953. Besides her family and friends, her main passion in life was making America more literate. She founded the Barbara Bush Foundation for Family Literacy in 1989. She wrote four books: *C. Fred's Story*; *Millie's Book*; *Barbara Bush: A Memoir*; and *Reflections: Life After the White House*. She died on April 17, 2018, at her home in Houston, Texas, with her husband of seventy-three years holding her hand.

Bush, Barbara, Jr.: Daughter of George and Laura Bush, she is the co-founder and board chair of Global Health Corps, an organization that has mobilized, trained, and placed more than 1,000 young leaders to solve the world's most pressing health challenges. From 2009 to 2018, she served as GHC's CEO, scaling their operations across five countries and a multitude of disease areas. She and her twin sister, Jenna, co-authored the number one *New York Times* best seller *Sisters First: Stories from Our Wild and Wonderful Life,* in 2017; the children's version was released in the fall of 2019. Barbara is currently enrolled at Harvard University's Kennedy School, pursuing her master's in public administration. She and her husband, Craig, live in Boston.

Bush, George Prescott: Son of Jeb and Columba Bush, he was elected land commissioner of Texas in 2014 and reelected to a second term in 2018. Prior to running for office, he was a public school teacher, a business-man, and served in Operation Enduring Freedom in Afghanistan as an officer in the US Naval Reserve. He lives in Austin, Texas, with his wife, Amanda, and two sons.

Bush, George W.: Oldest son of George and Barbara Bush, he was elected president of the United States in November 2000 and reelected in 2004. He served as governor of Texas from 1994 until stepping down to become president. Before entering politics, he was a businessman and co-managing partner of the Texas Rangers baseball team. Now an author and artist and an active participant at the George W. Bush Institute in Dallas, he is an avid mountain biker and golfer. He and his wife, Laura, live in Dallas and are the parents of two daughters and grandparents of three.

Bush, James: Son of President Bush's oldest brother, Prescott, and Elizabeth Kauffman Bush, Jamie is founder and CEO of Bush & Company, which specializes in business and family succession planning as well as corporate benefits and retirement planning. They also help families with children with special needs figure out what resources may be available to them. He and his wife, Sue, live in Hingham, Massachusetts, and are the parents of two children and grandparents of four.

Bush, John Ellis, Sr. (Jeb): Second son of George and Barbara Bush, he was governor of Florida from 1999 to 2007. He is honorary chair of the George H. W. Bush Library's board of trustees. Active in business and education reform and author of multiple books, he and his wife, Columba, live in Miami, the parents of three and grandparents of four.

Bush, John Ellis, Jr. (Jeb): Son of Columba and Jeb Bush, he works in venture capital and private equity. He contributes his time to a number of causes, including the Barbara Bush Foundation for Family Literacy, KIPP, and the National Alliance for Public Charter Schools. He and his wife, Sandra, live with their two daughters in Miami, Florida.

Bush, Josephine (Jody): Married to President Bush's brother Jonathan; the couple splits their time between Maine, Florida, and New York. They are the parents of two sons and grandparents of nine.

Bush, Laura: First Lady of the United States from 2001 until 2009, and the First Lady of Texas from 1995 until 2000, she worked as a public school teacher and librarian before marrying her husband, George W. Bush, in 1977. For decades she has championed key issues in the fields of education, health care, and human rights and today chairs the Women's Initiative at the George W. Bush Institute. The author of the best-selling memoir *Spoken from the Heart*, and co-author of the children's book *Our Great Big Backyard*, she co-founded both the Texas Book Festival and the National Book Festival.

Bush, Margaret: Wife of Marvin Bush, Margaret is a stage actress and has been performing from Maine to Florida for more than twenty years. For eight years she has been a trustee of the Maine Medical Center, home of the Barbara Bush Children's Hospital. She also is a floral designer and was inspired to take up needlepoint by her mother-in-law a decade ago.

Bush, Marvin: The fourth son of George and Barbara Bush, Marvin is a managing partner of Winston Partners, an investment firm in Arlington, Virginia. Marvin serves on the board of the George & Barbara Bush Foundation and is a past board member of the George W. Bush Presidential Library Foundation. He is currently on the board of the Virginia Athletic Foundation and is a past member of the board of managers of the University of Virginia Alumni Association and the board of trustees of the College Foundation of the University of Virginia. He and his wife, Margaret, live in Arlington, Virginia, and are the parents of a daughter and a son.

Bush, Neil: The third son of George and Barbara Bush, he is engaged in international business development with a focus on Asia. He is active in promoting Bush family charitable legacies, serving as chairman of the board of Points of Light; founder and chairman, with his wife, Maria, of the Barbara Bush Houston Literacy Foundation; and on the boards of the Bush School of Government and Public Service, the George & Barbara Bush Foundation, and the George H. W. Bush Foundation for US-China Relations. He and Maria live in Houston and are the parents of six and grandparents of two.

Bush, Noelle: The daughter of Jeb and Columba Bush, she lives in Orlando, Florida, where she is an operations assistant at the law firm Nelson Mullins. She loves yoga and the mountains.

Bush, Pierce George Mallon: Son of Neil and Sharon Bush, he is CEO of Big Brothers Big Sisters Lone Star, the largest Big Brothers Big Sisters affiliate agency in the country and the single largest one-to-one youth mentoring organization in the world. He lives in Houston with his wife, Sarahbeth, and their golden retriever, Winston Moose, an Instagram star.

Ellis, Robin Rand: Robin Ellis is married to Alexander (Hap) Ellis, whose mother is Nancy Bush Ellis, President Bush's only sister. She and her husband live in Boston and Kennebunkport and have three sons and eight grandchildren. She feels blessed to have been a member of the Ellis-Bush family for more than forty-five years.

Field, Betsy Walker: A first cousin of President Bush, she is the daughter of Grace and Louis Walker, youngest brother of President Bush's mother. She and her husband, John, raised their family in Barbara Bush's hometown of Rye, New York. They now reside in Wilmington, Delaware, and are the parents of two sons and grandparents of three.

Hager, Jenna Bush: Daughter of George W. and Laura Bush, Jenna is co-host of *Today with Hoda and Jenna*, the fourth hour of NBC's morning news program. She is the author of four books: *Ana's Story: A Journey of Hope*; with her mother, two children's books: *Read All About It!* and *Our Great Big Backyard*; and with her twin sister, Barbara, *Sisters First: Stories from Our Wild and Wonderful Life*; the children's version was released in the fall of 2019. Jenna and her husband, Henry, live in New York City with their three children.

Koch, Doro Bush: Youngest child of George and Barbara Bush, she is the co-founder of BB&R Wellness Consulting; the honorary chairman of the Barbara

Bush Foundation for Family Literacy; and a member of the board of the George & Barbara Bush Foundation. She is the author of *My Father, My President*. She and her husband, Bobby, live in Bethesda, Maryland, and have four children.

Koch, Gigi: Daughter of Doro and Bobby Koch, she lives in Washington, DC, where she works at a nonprofit called WEConnect International. She loves being outdoors and spending time with her family in Maine.

Koch, Robert: Son of Doro and Bobby Koch, he lives in Chatham, New Jersey, where he works as a sales consultant for Gallo Wine Sales of New Jersey. He is an avid Washington Redskins fan, and, with his brother Sam, is always first in line to enter the tailgate area for home games.

Lauren, Lauren Bush: Daughter of Neil and Sharon Bush, she is the founder and CEO of FEED, a social business with a mission to create good products that help feed the world. Over the last ten years, FEED has been able to provide more than 100 million meals to kids around the world. Lauren lives in New York City with her husband, David, and two sons.

LeBlond, Sam: Son of Doro Koch and Billy LeBlond, he is the regional director of safety and wellness at Reyes Holdings, LLC. He serves on the board of directors of the George & Barbara Bush Foundation and hosts the *All the Best* podcast, which promotes the legacy of his grandparents and service to others. He lives in Washington, DC, with his wife, Lee.

McCall, Louisa: A niece of President Bush, she is the daughter of Patty and William "Bucky" Bush, President Bush's youngest brother. She grew up in St. Louis, Missouri, and now lives in Greenwich, Connecticut, with her husband, Christian, and three children.

Pierce, Scott and Janice: Scott Pierce is Mrs. Bush's youngest brother and only surviving sibling. When he retired, he was chairman and CEO of PAMCO, the Prudential Asset Management Company. He was chairman of the board of Manhattanville College for eight years. He and his wife, Janice, have been married for more than sixty-five years and split their time between Yarmouth, Maine, and Amelia Island, Florida. They have four children, ten grandchildren, and three great-grandchildren. Scott had a five-dollar bet with his sister on who would die first. His nephew Neil gave him the five dollars at Mrs. Bush's funeral.

Sosa, Ellie LeBlond: Daughter of Doro Koch and Billy LeBlond, she lives in the Washington, DC, area with her husband, Nick, where she works in health and wellness. She is the author of *George and Barbara Bush: A Great American Love Story.*

Stapleton, Debbie Walker: A first cousin of President Bush, she is the daughter of Louis and Grace Walker. She served with her husband, Craig, overseas when he was ambassador to the Czech Republic and then France during the second Bush administration. Debbie serves on a variety of nonprofit boards and lives in Greenwich, Connecticut. She and Craig are the parents of two and grandparents of six. Debbie's full name is Dorothy Bush Walker Stapleton, having been named for President Bush's mother, Dorothy Walker Bush.

CHAPTER 2

Allen, Duane: Lead singer for the Oak Ridge Boys, he was a college student when he first campaigned for President Bush in the 1960s. The Oaks traveled with President Bush during all of his campaigns, and at his request, sang "Amazing Grace" at his funeral service in Houston. He and his wife, Norah Lee, live in

Nashville, Tennessee, the parents of two children and grandparents of four.

Appleby, Jim: As a high schooler, Jim began working as a "yard lad"—President Bush's job description—for the Bushes in Kennebunkport in 2001. He eventually became President Bush's personal aide, serving from 2006 until 2012. Today Jim works for Shell in external relations. He and his wife, Lauri, live in Houston with their two children.

Baker, James A., III, and Susan: James Baker served as secretary of state from 1989 to 1992, and also was Ronald Reagan's White House chief of staff and secretary of the Treasury. He is the only known person to lead five presidential campaigns for three different people. The author of numerous books and chairman of various boards and committees, he is an active participant in the James A. Baker III Institute of Public Policy at Rice University. He and his wife, Susan—a longtime volunteer and advocate for the homeless—live in Houston. Between them, they have eight children, nineteen grandchildren, and three great-grandchildren.

Bates, David: President Bush's personal aide from 1978 until 1981. He served President Bush in a variety of roles during the vice presidency and presidency, including assistant to the president and secretary to the cabinet and deputy to the chief of staff. From 1994 to 2009, he was managing director and then senior adviser for Public Strategies, Inc., a strategic consulting firm. He now is CEO of his own consulting company. He and his wife, Ann, live in San Antonio, the parents of three and grandparents of two.

Beach, Becky Brady: Aide to Barbara Bush from 1978 to 1981. She lives in Des Moines, Iowa, with her husband, Charlie, where she is CEO of the Puppy Jake Foundation. They have two children and six grandchildren.

Benedi, Antonio: Worked in a variety of roles during President Bush's vice presidency, including as an advance lead and events coordinator. Was deputy director of the Office of Appointments and Scheduling during the first Bush administration and continued to serve as an advance person after President Bush left the White House. He is a member of the board and past chairman of the Washington Regional Transplant Community. He and his wife, Maria, live in Springfield, Virginia, and are the parents of two sons and grandparents of one.

Blanton, Taylor: Worked as a volunteer in President George H. W. Bush's first two campaigns—for the US Senate in 1964 and the House of Representatives in 1966. He is retired from the US State Department and runs an event business in the Rio Grande Valley of Texas with his wife, Martha.

Brock, Ann: Director of scheduling for First Lady Barbara Bush. Right after leaving the White House, she served as the assistant director of the George H. W. Bush Presidential Library Foundation and director of the library's dedication ceremonies. She now lives in Jackson, Mississippi, where she is a middle school art teacher at St. Andrew's Episcopal School.

Brunette, Neely: Aide to Mrs. Bush from 2017 until she died in April 2018. She now lives in New York City and is an executive assistant at Burch Creative Capital.

Buckley, Christopher: A best-selling author and political satirist, Christopher (or Christo, as President Bush called him) was Vice President George Bush's speechwriter from 1981 until 1983. He and his wife, Katy, live in Stamford, Connecticut.

Card, Andrew: Served as White House chief of staff under President George W. Bush from 2001 to 2006. He was deputy White House chief of staff under the first President Bush before being named secretary of transportation in 1992. He got his start in politics serving in the Massachusetts House of Representatives from 1975 to 1983. His post–White House career has included serving as acting dean of the Bush School of Government and Public Service at Texas A&M University before becoming president of Franklin Pierce University in Rindge, New Hampshire, resigning in 2016. He and his wife, Kathleene, live in Jaffrey, New Hampshire, and have three children and six grandchildren.

Cary, Mary Kate: A speechwriter for President George H. W. Bush, she continues to write speeches for corporate and political clients. She was the producer of *41on41*, a CNN documentary about President Bush. She and her husband, Rob, live in Washington, DC, and are the parents of two daughters.

Cheney, Peter G.: He has served since 2002 as priest and chaplain of St. Ann's Episcopal Church, a summer chapel in Kennebunkport, Maine. He is the retired executive director of the National Association of Episcopal Schools. He and his wife, Kiki, split their time between Maine and Arizona.

Collamore, Tom: He leads the work of the George & Barbara Bush Foundation in Washington, DC. Tom worked for the George Bush for President campaign in Connecticut in 1979 and 1980. He then served in the twelve years of the Reagan and Bush administrations in various senior positions, including assistant to Vice President Bush and assistant secretary of commerce and chief of staff. Tom has served as head of global public affairs for a Fortune 10 company and head of communications for the US Chamber of Commerce. Tom and his wife, Jacqueline, have four children and live in Chevy Chase, Maryland.

Cooke, Julie: An assistant to Mrs. Bush during her husband's vice presidency, she was director of projects for the First Lady from 1989 to 1992. She recently retired from the Washington National Cathedral and volunteers as an English as a second language teacher in Washington, DC, where she lives with her husband, Tom. They are the parents of two sons and grandparents of two.

Crawford, Quincy Hicks: An aide to Barbara Bush from 1994 to 1998, she was director of scheduling and advance for First Lady Laura Bush from 2001 to 2002. She lives in New Orleans with her husband, JT, and their two sons. She does public relations and communications contract work as well as volunteer work for various organizations and businesses.

Cutler, Kim Brady: Aide to Barbara Bush from 1981 to 1985, Kim served in a variety of roles for the Bushes over the years, sometimes as a volunteer and sometimes paid. She was director of advance for the First Lady from 1989 to 1991. She's now a full-time volunteer and mother of two, and lives in Manchester, Massachusetts, with her husband, Nick.

Dannenhauer, Michael: Michael began working for Vice President Bush in 1985 at the age of seventeen, volunteering in the file room. He returned to Washington every summer to work in various vice presidential and White House offices, becoming President Bush's last White House personal aide and moving to Texas with the Bushes in 1993. He continued as Bush's personal aide for five years, then was his chief of staff for two, followed by a year at the George H. W. Bush Presidential Library Foundation. Michael returned to Washington to work in the second Bush administration, where he still resides today working as a Realtor.

DeLorenzo, Dante: Started working for President and Mrs. Bush in 2016 at their summer home in Kennebunkport as a yard lad. He currently still works for the Bush family. He attends the University of New Haven, where he is majoring in homeland security and emergency management and plays football. He is from Kennebunk, Maine.

Doublet, Elizabeth Wise: Aide to Mrs. Bush from 1985 to 1987. After a time living overseas as a foreign correspondent, she now lives in Washington, DC, with her husband, Jean-Louis, and their two sons.

Fenton, Cathy: She was deputy social secretary under Laurie Firestone in the first Bush administration and White House social secretary at the beginning of the second Bush administration. From 2010 to 2018 she was director of the governor's mansion for New Jersey governor Chris Christie and First Lady Mary Pat Christie. She is currently assistant chief of protocol for the US State Department. She and her husband, Tim, live in Washington, DC, and are the parents of one son.

Firestone, Laurie: She was Mrs. Bush's social secretary at the vice president's house for eight years before becoming White House social secretary for all four years of the first Bush administration. She lives in San Francisco, where she manages apartments. She has four children and thirteen grandchildren.

Gates, Robert M.: Served as the twenty-second secretary of defense (2006–2011) and is the only secretary of defense in US history to be asked to remain in that office by a newly elected president. Gates worked for eight presidents and has been heard commenting that President George H. W. and First Lady Barbara Bush's White House was the most fun. Before becoming secretary of defense in 2006, Gates was the president of Texas A&M University and before that served as interim dean of the George Bush School of Government and Public Service at Texas A&M from 1999 to 2001, and before that was director of the Central Intelligence Agency. The author of numerous books, he and his wife, Becky, live in Sedro-Woolley, Washington, and have two children.

Guerin, Dava: Author of numerous books, she is the former communications director for the US Association of Former Members of Congress. She has been an active participant in the Barbara Bush Foundation for Family Literacy, including helping to relaunch Mrs.

Bush's "Storytime." She lives with her two dogs on the Eastern Shore of Maryland.

Haley, Sondra: She launched her public affairs career in Vice President Bush's press office, and from 1983 until 1993 Sondra served in a variety of roles, including Barbara Bush's 1988 campaign spokesperson and deputy press secretary to the First Lady from 1989 until 1993. She currently is a communications consultant, living in her hometown of Seal Beach, California.

Hatcher, Teri: An actress, singer, and author, Teri is a veteran of numerous television shows but is best known for playing Lois Lane on *Lois and Clark: The New Adventures of Superman,* which aired on ABC from 1993 until 1997; and as Susan Mayer on ABC's *Desperate Housewives,* from 2004 until 2012. She lives in Los Angeles.

Heminway, Betsy: Betsy and her late husband, Spike, were among the Bushes' closest friends. They lived in Kennebunkport in the summer and Hobe Sound, Florida, in the winter. Betsy still does. She was active in President Bush's campaigns, serving in Connecticut as co-chair of '84 Reagan-Bush, and '88 and '92 Bush-Quayle. She has one daughter and two grandchildren.

Higgins, Hutton Hinson: Aide to Barbara Bush from 2010 to 2014. She currently serves as the senior development director for the Hope and Healing Center in Houston, where she lives with her husband, Taylor, and their daughter.

Huang, Nancy: Aide to Barbara Bush from 1993 to 1994. Worked in the White House as West Wing receptionist and Oval Office staff assistant. She currently is the chief of staff for Draper Richards Kaplan Foundation, a venture philanthropy firm that funds and supports early-stage social enterprises around the world. She lives in Truckee, California, with her husband, Dan, three kids, and two dogs.

Kaufman, Ron: In the first Bush White House, Ron was deputy assistant to the president for personnel and then deputy assistant for politics and White House political director. He started working for the Bushes in 1977 and gave them political advice for the rest of their lives. Currently senior strategic adviser to Dentons worldwide, he lives in Washington, DC, and is the father of two daughters and the grandfather of five.

Killblane, Casey Healey: Aide to Barbara Bush from 1987 until 1989. She left Barbara Bush only to marry her husband, Hugh. They live in Davis, Oklahoma, where they have an oil and gas investment company and a property management company, in addition to helping manage the family ranch, Flying L. Ranch. They have two sons.

Levenson, Russell J., Jr., and Laura: Reverend Levenson is the rector of St. Martin's Church in Houston, the largest Episcopal parish in the United States. He officiated at both President and Mrs. Bush's funerals. Laura is leader of the Christian Life Study Music Ministry at St. Martin's. They have three children and two grandchildren.

Major, John and Norma: Prime minister of the United Kingdom and Northern Ireland from 1990 until 1997, Sir John received in 2005 a Knight Companion of the Most Noble Order of the Garter—England's highest award for chivalry. He was a member of Parliament from 1979 until 2001 and served in Margaret Thatcher's cabinet in several capacities. Since leaving office, he has become patron or president of a number of international charities, including serving as chairman of the Queen Elizabeth Diamond Jubilee Trust. Norma was created a Dame Commander of the British Empire in recognition of her charitable work. They have two children and three grandchildren and split their time between London, Huntingdon, and North Norfolk.

McBride, Anita: Anita served in the White House as personnel director for Presidents Ronald Reagan and George H. W. Bush, as well as special assistant to the president for management and administration and as an assistant to President George W. Bush, and chief of staff to First Lady Laura Bush. Currently she is executive-in-residence in the School of Public Affairs at American University. McBride is on several boards, including the White House Historical Association, the Fulbright Foreign Scholarship Board, the Laura W. Bush Women's Initiative, and the National Symphony Orchestra. She and her husband, Tim, live in Washington, DC, and are the parents of two.

McBride, Tim: Serving President Bush in a variety of roles, he was his personal aide from 1985 until 1990. In 1990, the United States Senate confirmed McBride as assistant secretary of commerce for trade development. He later returned to the White House as assistant to the president for management and administration. He is currently senior vice president of government relations for United Technologies.

McEntire, Reba: A country music superstar, Reba has sold more than fifty-six million albums worldwide; is a member of the Country Music Hall of Fame; and has won dozens of music awards, including two Grammys and seven Country Music Awards. She was the star and producer of her own television series, *Reba*, and also starred on Broadway in *Annie Get Your Gun*. At President Bush's request, she sang the Lord's Prayer at his funeral in Houston. She lives in Nashville and has one son and several stepchildren and step-grandchildren.

Meacham, Jon: A presidential historian, best-selling author, and professor at Vanderbilt University, Jon's biographies include *Destiny and Power: The American Odyssey of George Herbert Walker Bush*. In 2009, he won the Pulitzer Prize for *American Lion: Andrew Jackson in the White House*. He and his wife, Keith, live in Nashville, Tennessee, with their three children.

Nevins, Kristan King: An aide to Barbara Bush from 2006 to 2008, she went on to serve at the Central Intelligence Agency, as chief of staff to Second Lady Karen Pence, and as a chief of staff in the House of Representatives. Kristan currently serves as the White House cabinet secretary and lives in Washington, DC, with her husband, Kyle, and three children.

O'Neil, Ashley: Ashley and her husband, Pierce, a lifelong friend of the Bush family, split their time between Maine and Palm Beach, Florida, where Ashley is a real estate agent with Brown Harris Stevens. They have three daughters and one dog.

Peressutti, Gian-Carlo: An aide to President Bush from 1996 to 2000, he currently is vice president of global communications at PepsiCo. He lives in Ridgefield, Connecticut, with his wife, Amanda (whom he met on the job in Kennebunkport), and two daughters.

Petersmeyer, Gregg: A longtime Bush family friend, Gregg is the founder and CEO of Personal Pathways, an early-stage enterprise software company. In President Bush's White House, he was assistant to the president and the founding director of the White House Office of National Service, taking President Bush's idea of a "Thousand Points of Light" and making it a reality. He was the lead architect of the Presidents' Summit for America's Future in 1997, out of which was created America's Promise. He and his wife, Julie, live in Bethesda, Maryland, and are the parents of four and grandparents of six.

Plumlee, Catherine Branch: Catherine was an aide to Barbara Bush from 2014 to 2017. She now resides in Dallas with her husband, Daniel, and works as a legal recruiter for Vinson & Elkins LLP.

Portman, Rob: Elected from Ohio in 2010, Senator Portman also was a congressman for twelve years, and held two cabinet-level jobs in the second Bush administration. He got his start in public service working for his mentor and role model, George H. W. Bush, first as a volunteer advance person and campaign coordinator in Ohio, then as associate counsel and deputy assistant and director of the Office of Legislative Affairs in the first Bush administration. He and his wife, Jane, live in Cincinnati, Ohio, and are the parents of three children.

Quayle, Dan: He became the 44th vice president of the United States under President George Herbert Walker Bush on January 20, 1989, having previously served in both the House of Representatives and the Senate from Indiana. He is chairman of Cerberus Global Investments, with more than thirty billion dollars under management. He and his wife, Marilyn, live in Scottsdale, Arizona, and have three children and eight grandchildren.

Rose, Susan Porter: Susan was chief of staff to Barbara Bush for twelve years, throughout the vice presidency and White House years. Previously she had served both First Ladies Pat Nixon and Betty Ford in a variety of roles. She and her husband, Jonathan, live in Alexandria, Virginia, and have one son.

Sanders, Kara Babers: Kara was an aide to Barbara Bush from 1998 to 2000. She lives in Houston with her husband, Dax, where she loves being a stay-at-home mom to their two daughters and dog, Maggie.

Sheldon, Brooke: Aide to Mrs. Bush from 2000 to 2003, she spends her summers in Kennebunkport.

Sherzer, Amanda Aulds: Aide to Barbara Bush from 2008 to 2010. A graduate of Dallas Theological Seminary, she is a writer, a wife to David, and a mother to three young children. She lives with her family in Colleyville, Texas.

Stanton, Michele Whalen: Aide to Mrs. Bush from 2003 to 2006. Served as a presidential appointee for George W. Bush in the commissioner's office of the Food and Drug Administration from 2006 to 2008. She lives in College Station, Texas, with her husband, Clay, and their two daughters. She still works for former FDA commissioner Andrew C. von Eschenbach, as well as volunteers for various organizations, including the George & Barbara Bush Foundation.

Untermeyer, Charles (Chase): He was a volunteer in the 1966 Bush for Congress campaign and afterward spent two summers as an intern in Congressman Bush's Washington office. He was executive assistant to Vice President Bush; director of presidential personnel and director of the Voice of America under the first President Bush; and US ambassador to Qatar under the second. The author of several books, he currently is an international business consultant. He and his wife, Diana, whom he met in the White House, live in Houston and have one daughter.

Updegrove, Mark and Amy: Mark, a presidential historian and author, is president and CEO of the LBJ Foundation. His book *The Last Republicans*, about the two President Bushes, was released in 2017. Mark lives in Austin, Texas, with Amy and their four children. Amy is an Austin-based media and marketing executive.

White, Peggy Swift: Aide to Barbara Bush from 1989 to 1993. After a career in public relations, corporate communications, and project management, Peggy dedicates her time as a civic volunteer and lives with her husband, Brian, in Chicago.

Pearls of Wisdom

Pearls of Wisdom

CHAPTER 1

Family First

Mom has taught me to be a better parent, a better person, and a better citizen.

—Neil Bush

What better place to start with the wit and wisdom of Barbara Bush than with her family. They were, after all, the very essence of her life.

In her nearly ninety-three years of giving advice—yes, she no doubt started in the womb by delivering her mother a kick or two—she most certainly showered her children and grandchildren with more advice than any other group of people. How to eat, how to dress, how to behave, how to make their bed, whom to date. They rarely needed to wonder just where their mother/Ganny stood on most matters.

So it was with some surprise to her children that when their mom published her memoirs in 1994, she included a letter she had written them in the spring of 1993 but had never mailed. Why? She just didn't think it was proper. This was news to them. Here is what she had written:

It was one night about this time that I absolutely couldn't sleep, and I got to thinking about what I have learned in life—sometimes the hard way—and the advice I'd like to give my precious children, if I could or would. I found myself at the computer composing a letter, which I never sent but would like to share with you now:

I can think of no better lesson to teach you than to try—and oh boy, how hard it is—to always find the good in people and not the bad. I remember many years ago that I wasted so much time worrying about my mother. I suffered because she and I had a "chemical thing." I loved her very much but was hurt by her. (I am sure that I hurt her a lot, too.) Grace Walker[1] said to me once, "Think of all the lovely things about your mother, all the things you love and are proud of about her." There were so many that I couldn't count them all. I think that I expected her to

---

1   Grace Walker was married to President George H. W. Bush's uncle Lou Walker, his mother's youngest brother.

be perfect. Nobody is perfect. Certainly not me. So LOOK FOR THE GOOD IN OTHERS. Forget the other.

Clara Barton, founder and president of the Red Cross, was once reminded of a wrong a friend had done to her years earlier. "Don't you remember?" the friend asked. "No," replied Clara firmly. "I distinctly remember forgetting that." Not bad advice. Take a lesson from your dad. He says when I remind him that someone has been hateful, "Isn't it better to make a friend rather than an enemy?" He's right, too.

Don't talk about money—either having it or not having it. It is embarrassing for others and quite frankly vulgar.

DO NOT BUY SOMETHING THAT YOU CANNOT AFFORD. YOU DO NOT NEED IT.

If you really need something and can't afford it, for heaven's sake call home. That's what family are all about.

Do not try to live up to your neighbors. They won't look down on you if you don't have two television sets. They will look down on you if you buy things that you cannot afford, and they will know it! They are only interested in their possessions, not yours.

Be sure that you pay people back. If you have

dinner at their house or they take you out, have them back, but remember you don't need the expensive thing. You can make the best spaghetti in the world. People love to come to your home. Plan ahead and it will be fun.

Value your friends. They are your most valuable asset.

Remember loyalty is a two-way street. It goes up and down. So be loyal to those people who are loyal to you. Your dad is the best example of two-way loyalty that I know.

Love your children. I don't have to tell any of you that. You are the best children any two people ever had. I know you will be as lucky. Your kids are great. Dad and I love them more than life itself. I think you know that about your dad. I do also.

Remember what Robert Fulghum says: "Don't worry that your children never listen to you; worry that they are always watching you."

For heaven's sake enjoy life. Don't cry over things that were or things that aren't. Enjoy what you have now to the fullest. In all honesty you really only have two choices: You can like what you do OR you can dislike it. I choose to like it, and what fun I have had. The other choice is no fun and people do not want to be around a whiner. We can always find people who

are worse off, and we don't have to look far! Help them and forget yourself!

I would certainly say, above all, seek God. He will come to you if you look. There is absolutely NO downside. Please expose your children and set a good example for them by going to church. We, your dad and I, have tried to live as Christian a life as we can. We certainly have not been perfect. Maybe you can be! Keep trying.

More than twenty years later, in honor of her ninetieth birthday, her five children wrote essays about their mom, specifically about what they had learned from her. You could say it was their turn.

Here are their essays, in order of their birth:

George W. Bush:

Barbara Bush taught us how to live, love, and laugh. When asked whether she would be willing to uproot her young family and leave the comforts of Greenwich, Connecticut, she did not hesitate. She, of course, would say that she would go anywhere with the love of her life, our dad. I think it was more than that. I think she, too, has an adventuresome spirit; and the idea of heading to the foreign culture of West Texas intrigued her. She was not fearful of change. This was a pattern

of her life. She, of course, was not the one who was offered the new challenges; but she was the one who charged ahead with no complaints and an eagerness to learn. Like her mate, she felt life was to be lived to the max. I smile when I think of Mom and her little yelpers (those would be her dogs) walking the beach in Kennebunkport with the aid of a walker. Her message is walk life's beaches for as long as you can.

Mom taught us how to love. No doubt her number one love was Dad. But she had plenty of love to spare for her children. She was always encouraging and never deflating (except the time she told me that I couldn't beat Ann Richards for governor of Texas). She was the disciplinarian in our family. She was quick to scold when I stepped over the imaginary good behavior line. She spoke her mind. There was not much subtlety. But once the tempest passed, she was quick to move on. She did so because of the love in her heart.

Mom has a sharp and quick wit. She is not afraid to speak her mind. She is self-deprecating. She can spot a phony before most. She deflated the pompous and the arrogant. She is a pro at putting people at ease because she herself is at ease. On her dog walks she befriends all kinds of people. The local tomato salesman is one of her favorites. Of course she remembered the name of every dog. During my time in office, the number of

people who said "I just love your mother," or "I wish I could just meet your mother" was astounding.

Mom taught me how to laugh, how to see irony, how to verbally joust. She had a door mat in our home in Houston that said "Birds fly high because they take themselves lightly." She always took her duties seriously, like that of First Lady. But never herself.

I could go on and on, but she might think that I was the pompous one. So I end knowing that I'm a lucky man to have had Barbara Bush as a mother.

Jeb Bush:

We could all use a good dose of Barbara Bush's humor, her caring, and her plain-spoken wisdom. I say that as a totally biased son but am willing to wager that there are millions who would agree with that sentiment.

Barbara Pierce Bush is an American treasure.

As to what she has taught me, I would start with how to be a good parent. Mom has always had the firm belief that a successful life is defined first and foremost by loving your children with all of your heart and soul. How lucky we were to learn the habits that lead to a successful life from the best!

Mom did that. One of my earliest childhood memories is reading books chronicling the adventures of Babar the Elephant with her. Later it was Zelda the Zebra. I loved the pictures, and together we read those books hundreds of times—by which time I am sure Mom could recite each book from memory. Still, it was one of her first, and most important, gifts to me: the gift of reading.

The time she invested in us and the power of her example inspired me when my wife, Columba, and I were blessed with three wonderful children of our own.

Mom taught me plenty of other things as well. She taught me the importance of civility. She taught me not to take myself seriously. God help you if she ever caught you acting arrogant. You would get that Barbara Bush look and then you would be hit with her very quick and sharp wit that would put you in your place. Even today, when I am speaking to an audience, I feel her looming presence behind me whispering: **Don't brag. Don't toot your own horn too loud. Don't talk like a big shot.**

Dad calls Mom "The Enforcer," because she tends to be the one who has meted out discipline through the years. Like many parents, my mother's style of discipline could often be fairly described as a benevolent dictatorship. But if you had really messed up, she could just as readily discard the benevolent part. Looking back, however, I have to confess the punishment usually fit the crime.

Long before I ever considered entering politics, Mom also taught us the importance of staying on message. If Mom ever gave you advice or corrected you, she was apt to repeat herself. On this front, my siblings and I challenged her patience on a regular basis. Still, hearing her impart the same pearl of wisdom repeatedly became the first known instance of a phenomenon today called "Bush fatigue."

I suppose it would have helped things had we been faster learners, or better behaved.

Aside from family, Barbara Bush is the best friend to hundreds if not thousands of people. I imagine her time living in Washington taught her the true meaning of genuine friendship. Friends are with you through the good times and the bad ones too. She learned a lot about friendship after watching my sister Robin slip from their grasp at an innocent, early age. My parents will never forget the way their friends and neighbors in Midland rallied to their side.

Mom also taught us the importance of faith in God, but never in a preachy, showy kind of way. Again, it is in the consistent manner in which she has lived her life, reaching out to others, trying to leave this a better world than she found it.

Now, having said all of this, let me confide that Barbara Bush would be the first to tell you she is not perfect. As president, my brother George got us both in trouble at a Florida event during which he teased Mom about her lack of total expertise in the kitchen. (Mom didn't buy my explanation that I was laughing just to be polite to the president of the United States.) More recently, I have learned that she can be somewhat deficient in explaining *certain* political endorsements![2]

But where Mom is totally wrong is in describing herself as the luckiest person in the world. That simply cannot be, because it is us "kids," my siblings and I, who have been blessed beyond belief to have Barbara Pierce Bush raise us, and guide us, and instill in us a sense of values. Together with our father, she has given us the love and lessons we need to make our way in this complex and wonderful world.

Neil Bush:

It has been a joy to share America's mother with a nation that loves Barbara Bush. Mom's seventy-year devoted marriage, her public affection and support for her children and grandchildren, her sharp humor, her

---

2   When Jeb was considering running for president of the United States in 2016, his mother publicly discouraged him from doing so, announcing there had been "enough Bushes." She later recanted and enthusiastically supported his candidacy.

naturally elegant pearl-accented style and silver head of hair have endeared her to millions.

On a very personal basis, as a son, Mom has taught me to be a better parent, a better person, and a better citizen.

She has taught me to be a better parent by demonstrating the importance of unconditional love. I struggled with reading in elementary and middle school. Mom felt my pain and worked hard to find a diagnosis and solution. She stood by me, lifted my spirits, helped me find joy in things I did well, and made sure my life wasn't mired in self-doubt. There has never been a question about my mother's commitment to my health and well-being. She is a Neil Bush warrior, and I've learned to be a devoted and loving parent from her.

Mom has taught me to be a better person by demonstrating core values that ground good behavior, lead to wise choices, and make life a whole lot better.

Under her early leadership I learned to make my bed, to hang up used towels, and to use a bank account. She prepared me for living independently. Mom has also taught me to endure hardship.

Mom has endured indescribable back pain, rarely complaining. She doesn't burden other people with tales of her woes. After double knee replacement or heart valve surgery, she recovered quickly, demonstrating amazing willpower. I've learned from her to power through pain, to endure jet lag, to bounce up after a fall and to get back in the game.

She taught us to be kind and respectful of others, to say thank you, and to be polite. She praises hard work and good deeds. And Mom is the gatekeeper for grounding her large flock of children and grandchildren. There are no inflated egos or feelings of entitlement in the Bush family.

She advocates transparency and owning up to things. Oftentimes it has to do with spending money. As a young couple with a bunch of kids, Mom and Dad didn't spend money on exotic family trips. They always preferred to save. Mom fiercely advocates frugality and living a debt-free lifestyle. Also, I've learned that there is no point in hiding stuff; she will find out about the ski vacation in Colorado or beach trip to the Bahamas. I married a woman who shares Mom's aversion to debt, so at the age of sixty, I'm on the right track.

Truthfully, I'm still working to incorporate into my life some of the things that Mom has emphasized.

And finally, I am a better citizen because I've seen Mom's active commitment to helping others throughout her life. Before she had the First Lady's platform where her charitable works received lots of attention,

Mom would selflessly volunteer in hospitals, in schools, and in the communities where she lived. It's no wonder that service has become a part of the Bush family culture, and now I serve as chairman of Points of Light, the largest organization in the world focused on volunteerism. What ignites my passion more than anything is work we are doing in Houston through the Barbara Bush Houston Literacy Foundation.

It is a blessing to have a strong, stable, loving, witty mother in my life. She fills my heart with joy and blankets me with unconditional love and support. If every family were led by a Barbara Bush, the world would be a much better place.

Marvin Bush:

A few valuable lessons learned from my mom, Barbara Pierce Bush:

- **Be on time.**

I felt like a lottery winner in October of 1956 when I finally stuck my head out of Mom's womb and first laid eyes on that incredible woman. I've learned many lessons from her over the years, but the first one was impressed upon me on that day in October. The lesson? BE ON TIME! Apparently, she was raised to think that it was rude—and selfish—to keep people waiting, including herself, so she asked the doctor for a healthy dose of castor oil to expedite my birth at Midland Hospital. Lesson learned, Mom. Thanks to you I now get to social gatherings, airports, and business meetings with time to spare.

- **Be yourself.**

When I was little, I remember my mom changing her hair color so that she could appear younger than her premature gray hair suggested. Most of the shades were in the light to dark brown kaleidoscope, but one hairdresser left her with a color that could kindly be called "copper" or "rust." I think she looked in the mirror and didn't see a reflection that made her happy. I don't remember her saying a word about it, but a few weeks later, her hair was gray and there was once again an authenticity to her beauty.

My mom named me after her dad, Marvin Pierce. As a kid I would repeatedly tell her that I was the only guy I knew named Marvin and that no one has used the name since she and Dad unleashed it on me in the mid-1950s. Her response over the years varied from **your dad and I didn't want to waste that beautiful name on one of your other brothers** to **count your blessings; we were going to name you Maude if you were a girl.** Of course, now I see it her way. I'm honored to be named after her wonderful dad and have become very comfortable with the uniqueness of the name.

- **A sense of humor can be your friend.**

Mom will unanimously be inducted into the Self-Deprecating Humor Hall of Fame on the first ballot. I remember her response to a reporter who asked about the adjustments made after she and Dad left Washington and the White House:

It's been different. I started driving again. I started cooking again. My driving's better than my cooking. George has discovered Sam's Club.

She taught us all early that humor is a friend that can guide you out of the tightest jams or through the toughest times. When the "perfect storm" devastated Walker's Point in 1991, she and Dad went to Kennebunkport to survey the damage. Worried, I called Mom to see how they were holding up. Her enthusiastic response: **Great, Marv, the only valuable we found on the rocks was your high school picture!** That picture of me with unruly hair, an ugly blue jean jacket, and a snarl that would make any parent cringe became a running joke between us. Every time we visited Maine my mom would prominently display the picture, much to my protestation. She knew how much I hated the picture, but it brought her great joy that our running joke could continue.

- **Love one another.**

There wasn't a moment that I've been on this planet that I didn't feel really loved by Mom. Her loyalty to her kids is legendary. I wouldn't call it "blind love," but it was close. Let's call it "blurry-to-blind love." She gave a hug when one was needed, supported us through thick and thin, believed in us when we had our own doubts, and teased us when we needed what my dad calls "the needle." On the other hand, she was quick to discipline us when it was merited. We tested her like it was our day job and she responded like a mom who really loves her kids—with swift, consistent punishment.

Growing up we had a front-row seat at one of the greatest love stories that ever existed. My parents can't get enough of each other. Their love has grown stronger with each passing year. They laugh at each other's goofy jokes, hold hands when no one is around, and generally look at each other like teenagers in love. Being the offspring of my mom, I sometimes feel like saying, "Enough, you two, get a room." Knowing my mom, she would respond with something like: **I have a room and the best roommate in the world.**

Doro Bush Koch:

As the only daughter among my parents' five children, I have the unique designation of being the only woman in history to see both her father and her brother become president. While I feel honored to have this credential, I feel even more honored to be able to say that I am Barbara Bush's daughter.

The list is long when I consider everything I've learned from my remarkable and very colorful mother, so I might as well begin with the first thought that came to mind—Miss Rumphius. *Miss Rumphius* by Barbara Cooney is one of my mother's favorite children's books. It is no surprise that this was my first thought given my mom's love of reading and passion for literacy. In the book, Miss Rumphius is instructed by her grandfather to leave the world a better place. She decides to do so by spreading flower seeds wherever she goes in the hope that it will make the world more colorful, and thus, more beautiful. While my mother may not have spread actual flower seeds throughout the world, she certainly makes it a more colorful and beautiful place.

My mother is known for speaking her mind in the most unique and entertaining way possible. When I was growing up and I did something right, she might say something like, **That's using your head for something other than a hat rack!** On the other hand, if I did something she did not think was very bright, she would say, **Don't be a stupenagel**—whatever that means!

Mom is also known for saying things that she (at times) later regrets. Once there was a rather plumpish guest visiting our family in Maine and when my mom spotted him, she simply stated, **There's the whale up by the pool!** She always keeps us guessing about what she might say next! But the truth is, my mother's unpredictable and colorful language has led to a life filled with entertainment and joy.

My mother takes this colorful attitude and reflects it in her style as well. When she was given a collection of Keds sneakers in a rainbow of colors for her birthday, she wore them all with gusto. She even went one step further and mismatched them, strutting out in one green sneaker paired with a blue sneaker or a red one matched with a yellow one. People would often look at her sideways, wondering if this was on purpose or if Mom was beginning to lose it. The truth is, Mom relishes being playful and unapologetically being herself—two qualities that I try to emulate in my own life.

In her later years Mom dedicated herself to making the life of our dad more colorful. Through this, Mom has taught me to lead with love because that is what really matters. She has taught me the importance of

being present for one another, no matter how difficult the circumstance.

Ultimately, Mom has taught me to make the world a better place by filling it with color. My mother brings color to the world each day with her imaginative comments, her authentic style, her passion for literacy, and her unwavering loyalty.

She is our very own Miss Rumphius.

Mrs. Bush also, of course, gave loving advice to her grand-children, especially as they grew older. Just as she did with her own children, she did not want them to be spoiled and wanted them to take responsibility for their own lives.

A good place to start, she decided, was when they were visiting Walker's Point in Kennebunkport, Maine, the Bushes' summer home. She attached this set of rules to the back of every single bedroom door:

BUSH CHILDREN AND GRANDCHILDREN

1. **Please hang up damp towels and use twice if possible.**
2. **Try to make beds and keep room picked up; makes dusting and vacuuming easier.**
3. **Please collect your gear from around the house and keep it in your room.**

4. **If possible, let the kitchen know your meal plans:**

    - **Picnics**
    - **Specific requests for you or your children**
    - **Missing a meal**

5. **Breakfast served from 8 to 9 a.m.—coffee begins at 6:30 a.m. (It's really more like 5:30 a.m.!)**
6. **Please put dirty clothes outside your door every night.**
7. **Ask Paula[3] if you can help her.**
8. **Above all—have a great time. This is our happiest time of the year!**

However, even Mrs. Bush found that giving her grandchildren advice could be tricky as they grew older and often included in her speeches the "dos and don'ts" of having grandchildren in the house. This passage is from 2003:

For a few weeks we had six teenage grandchildren staying with us...now that was an adventure. Walker's Point was rocking. They all had friends, including a boyfriend or girlfriend or two, and

---

3 Paula Rendon, the Bushes' longtime housekeeper.

what's worse, they all came with driver's licenses. It made one yearn for the good old diaper and bottle days...

I was thinking about all this over the weekend, as I kept one eye on Hurricane Fabian and wondered if it would keep me from coming today. I was reminded of the story of the East Coast family, who when they heard a hurricane was coming their way, sent a telegram to a relative in the Midwest: "Hurricane coming and am sending children to you." In a few days, the relative sent a cable back: "Am returning children; send hurricane."

Anyway, we did learn a thing or two about having teenagers in the house and would like to share them with you today. Maybe I can help prevent you from making some of the mistakes we made with our grandchildren.

- Be careful of criticizing their clothes. What they change into could be tighter and shorter than what you made them take off.
- If you have a lot of tension and you get a headache, do what it says on the aspirin bottle: "Take two aspirin" and "Keep away from children."
- You can't hide a piece of broccoli in a glass of

milk. That would be funny if I were talking about a grandchild.[4]

In later versions of this advice, she added two more bullet points:

- **Don't lend your car to anyone you gave birth to or their offspring.**
- **If you can remain calm, you just don't have all the facts.**

And now, once again, it's their turn. Barbara Bush's grandchildren offered to share what they learned most from their Ganny, listed below in the order in which they did their homework. (Their Ganny would so approve of that logic.) To help avoid repetition, I will just say this once: Every single one of them included in their essay how much they loved their Ganny (and Gampy) and they were blessed to have such amazing grandparents.

George P. Bush:

Best advice she ever gave me was to actually **do something in your own right before thinking about**

---

4   President Bush famously hated broccoli.

22

politics. I've said this publicly before and people really appreciate her direct and candid advice at the time (I was in my twenties): **Be your own man—build a career, buy a house, pay taxes like everyone else—marry someone great.** I think her advice not only applies to a grandson thinking about career choices but really to any young person thinking about getting ahead.

Lizzie Andrews:

- **Have an opinion and be confident in that.**
- **Always have a good story.**

Many who were close with Ganny know that she always loved a good story. Whenever something fun and interesting came up, the first person my mom [Maria Bush] and I wanted to tell was Ganny. I think it was because she always had an opinion and we loved hearing it. That's one of the things that made her so special…Today, whenever I have a good story I still wonder, "What would Ganny say?"

Jeb Bush, Jr.:

Lessons from Ganny:

- **ALWAYS be grateful.**

- Look someone in the eyes when meeting them, with a firm handshake.
- Say "yes ma'am" when responding to her, or "yes sir" to Gampy, or to anyone your senior.
- Don't say "like" when trying to discuss something.
- Pick up your dirty laundry and wet towels. Make your bed.
- DO YOUR SUMMER READING!
- No elbows on the table.
- Do not leave the table until you have finished all your food. But don't overeat and ask for too much.
- Laugh.
- Don't be so quiet.
- Keep things in perspective, stay focused, and remember faith, family, and friends.
- Listen to your parents.
- Watch out for the blue-eyed one (referring to my youngest child).
- Hug your girls.
- Read. Read. Read.
- Listen. Learn. Lead.
- Say your blessings every night.

Ellie LeBlond Sosa:

The one lesson that sticks out the most is this: **Live your life with love as your guiding principle—keep your family and close friends close**. And show them that you love them. Ganny was never really one to lecture us grandkids with advice about life. She never really told us about the importance of family and close friends. But she lived her life accordingly, and we all watched and learned through her example.

My grandmother loved my grandfather more than anyone in the world, and a close second went to her children and grandchildren. We were included in everything with my grandparents, whether it was the Easter egg roll at the White House, a boat ride in Maine during the summer, or my grandfather's inauguration in 1989. We were all there every step of the way. And still today, we support each other no matter what, cry with each other, laugh A LOT, and most importantly, we love each and every single person in our large, sometimes wacky family. And that is all due in large part to Ganny and her example of love.

Lauren Bush Lauren:

My Ganny, Barbara Bush, was a strong matriarch whose pearls of wisdom were offered to all who knew her, but especially her grandkids, regularly and without hesitation. These candid "truths" were at times jarring, but always instructive and meant to make us the best version of ourselves. Here are a few that are forever etched in my memory, thanks to Ganny.

- **Don't say "um," "yeah," or "like."** Hence, speak clearly and precisely. (The unfortunate thing about this advice is that the more you are told not to say something, the more ingrained the words become.)
- **Be patient.** Ganny loved to garden in Maine. Once, I was walking by and picked a bud from her garden without thinking and was caught red-handed. Needless to say, Ganny was not happy. She marched me over to a beautiful flower in full bloom and told me that this is what this bud could have become. She loved to plant the seeds and watch them grow to their full beauty. Even now that she is gone, her garden in Maine is magnificent thanks to her tender and patient care year after year.
- **Stay current.** My grandmother was one of the first people I knew to get a BlackBerry, then a Kindle, then an iPhone, and eventually even an Instagram account featuring her beloved Bibi and Mini[5] as

---

5 Bibi and Mini Me were Mrs. Bush's last dogs, both Maltipoos. The name Bibi came from a nickname President Bush once had

her profile picture. And one summer when the Fitbit trend was at its height and she was well into her late eighties and not walking as much as she once did, she would wear it around her ankle to get extra "steps" when she rode her giant adult tricycle around the Point in Maine.

- **Be loyal**. My Ganny was loyal to my grandfather until the end. As they both got older, she would often say that she wanted to live one day longer than our Gampy. She wanted to be there for him, and when he was gone, she would be ready to go. The loyalty to her husband and her family clearly brought her so much joy and purpose in life. This unwavering loyalty made her at times a force to be reckoned with but also my greatest champion.

Sam LeBlond:

Ganny wrote this letter to my wife, Lee, and me on our first anniversary:

Happy Anniversary. I was asked for a little advice for a happy life—you two—really don't need it for

---

for his wife; Mini Me came from the fact Mini had all-white hair, making her—according to President Bush—a miniature version of Mrs. Bush.

you were brought up in happy homes. But most of all because you love and respect each other. But here is my advice: Each one of you should go 75 percent of the way and to remember to laugh.

Love from a Ganny who loves you both and Gampy.

Georgia (Gigi) Koch:

Ganny treated everyone the same. She wasn't impressed by titles, how fancy you were, where you came from, where you went to school, etc. Whether it be a family member or a stranger, she taught me the importance of treating everyone with kindness and respect.

She also taught us the importance of keeping family and friends close. My grandmother had more good friends than you can count, all of whom she remained close with up until her final days. Ganny was the glue in our family in a sense that she kept our entire family together, making sure everyone saw each other around Christmastime and in the summer. Family and friends bring laughter, love, and total ease. In our family, there is LOTS of laughter. Ganny's witty remarks and sharp humor kept our entire family laughing throughout her lifetime. I know that family was important to her because family will always be there no matter what— through the ups and downs in life.

Ganny told us that in her darkest times, having

family by her side, especially Gampy, helped her get through. I have no doubt that his humor played a role in helping her.

Noelle Bush:

I learned to be humble with others. She mentioned this before dropping me off in a limousine at elementary school. She always said I love you.

Robert Koch:

It was up in Maine where I learned many important life lessons. Through Ganny's gentle daily urging to complete our summer reading, I learned the importance of keeping an active mind. Ganny was always reading, needlepointing, or interacting with friends and family and she was sharp as a tack until the day that we lost her.

I also learned the importance of keeping active physically from Ganny, as she would swim lap after lap in the pool each day while my cousins and I jumped and played all around her. She was happy to have us there with her and we could swim all around as she freestyle stroked away. She would listen to books on tape while she exercised in the pool—how's that for an active mind and body?

One final pearl of wisdom I learned from my amazing grandmother was the importance of having good things in moderation, and this was a lesson she really had to hammer home with me. When I was but a "little wiener," as Gampy would say, around the age of eight or so, I was very fond of Klondike bars (still am). I would enjoy one after lunch, one after dinner, and maybe one as an afternoon snack after a day of running around outside. It got to the point where Ganny had to speak with me about cutting it way back. This didn't resonate with my eight-year-old brain, and one day, I snuck over to Ganny and Gampy's house to grab my afternoon Klondike to find, to my surprise, a PAD-LOCK on the freezer! The freezer now required a key to access all the delicious Klondike bars that lay within. This was a tough pill to swallow at the time, but truly hilarious as I look back.

Ashley Bush:

When I was little, I thought I was going to be the next Madonna. Unfortunately I was born tone deaf and have to wear hearing aids in both ears. My grandmother knew I loved singing and never wanted me to feel different because of this. She'd pack a room full of adults (some very generous donors) who'd all have to sit there and smile and applaud while I sang a very out-of-tune version of Louis Armstrong's "What a Wonderful World."

It was a small moment. But it made me feel normal and gave me the confidence to be whoever I wanted.

Ganny treated everyone as a normal person, and she expected to be treated the same way, too. Even in her old age, she refused any sort of help, any sort of special privilege.

And regardless of how busy she was, Ganny always knew the smallest details of what was going on with her kids and grandkids—which cousin was where and when and even what book they were reading.

And she loved gossip, so much so that she told me about my engagement before my fiancé did.

After she passed away, I was wandering around the more private rooms of her house. Places you might expect to find campaign memorabilia or fancy possessions, but instead there was nothing but these huge, handmade collages she had put together of her family. Some photos were faded with age, others were freshly printed. Photos of my cousins and me growing up, her kids—my dad and his siblings—her and Gampy on their wedding day, and her newest great-grandkids. No matter how extraordinary the events of her life were, she was always focused on the people around her.

Whether it was launching a program to get millions of people reading or arranging an impromptu concert for a little girl with hearing problems, she dedicated her life to the people around her. In Ganny's words: **Cherish your human connections—your relationships with family and friends.**

Pierce Bush:

There are so many pearls of wisdom I have learned by winning the proverbial lottery and being the grandson of Barbara Pierce Bush. I think the one I am most grateful for at this stage in my life was her relentless drive to make sure all her grandkids understood that working hard at whatever you did in life—and always trying your very best—are worthy character traits. I have a distinct memory of being a nine-year-old boy and getting hired by Ganny, with my slightly older cousins Jebby and Sam, to do some outdoor yard work in Kennebunkport on her beloved garden. It was incredibly hot outside and we were all slacking on the job, drinking Cokes and watching MTV inside trying to cool off, thinking Ganny was away and wouldn't know better. Out of nowhere we see Ganny's hat poking up through a window outside, looking in at us, and we decided foolishly to make a run for it and pretend like we were working the whole time. Being a person who NEVER let anything get by her, she caught us red-handed and gave all of us a lesson that was tough to take at the time but helped mold all of us into the people we are today. She never wanted any of her grandkids to take anything for granted and pushed us to value hard work, ideally on something that had larger purpose than pure self-gain. I feel my career in life is a product of how she drove these values into me, starting with that summer job so many years ago, and I will always treasure her wisdom.

Barbara Bush:

(Taken from the book Sisters First, *authored by Barbara and Jenna Bush Hager.)*

Since I was young, heading to Maine made me want to be my best self. Ganny was astute and picked up on shortcomings. She held us to high standards because she believed we could meet them, and because of her belief in us, we tried…She worried her name was burdensome to me, but rather it was emboldening. Carrying her name made me expect more—made me want to be more. More authentic, more fearless, more protective, and more loving—just the way she had been—even until the moment she left the earth.

Jenna Bush Hager:

(Taken from a "letter" she wrote to her grandmother after her death.)

We called you "The Enforcer." It was because, of course, you were a force and you wrote the rules and your rules were simple. **Treat everyone equally, don't look down on anyone, use your voices for good, read all the great books** (oh, how I will miss sharing books with you!).

From you, Ganny, I have learned the gift of uniqueness and authenticity, from wearing mixed Keds, to your signature pearls and snow-white hair. You taught us that humor, wit, and grace are the best accessories and that worrying too much about looks is (in your words) boring. **Words matter; kindness matters; looks fade.**

Mrs. Bush shined her guiding light on everyone in the extended Bush/Walker/Pierce family network. Here are some favorite nuggets from other beloved family members:

Daughter-in-law Laura Bush:

Bar seldom gave me advice; she knew that daughters-in-law didn't want advice from their mothers-in-law. But one time early in our marriage, when George was running for Congress in West Texas, she told me never to criticize my husband's speeches. She said she'd recently criticized her George's speech, and he'd come home for weeks afterward with letters saying it was the best speech he'd ever given.

So I took her advice, and I never criticized George's

speeches, until one evening when we were driving home from Lubbock to Midland.

Just as we turned into the driveway, George said, "Tell me the truth: How was my speech?" I told him the truth and he drove into the garage wall.

I should have listened to her advice.

Daughter-in-law Margaret Bush:

I learned so many things from Barbara Bush, but what I think of most is her perseverance.

She never quit, she pushed forward, no matter how difficult the task.

One summer in Maine she fell while working out on one of the machines in the gym on Walker's Point. The next day, the board of trustees of the Maine Medical Center (of which I was a member) was coming for a reception. Ganny had turned black and blue all over from her fall. She could have easily chosen to remain safely tucked away in her room while the guests had cocktails with Gampy and me.

Not Barbara Bush. Instead, she found the humor in it. Not only did she attend, but she wore signs around her neck to highlight the outrageous bruising that had discolored her entire body. She rotated them through-out the evening.

- **You should see the other guy.**
- **No, George didn't hit me.**
- **I'm trying out my Halloween costume.**

I will never forget the inner strength and persever-ance it took for her to be there for me and the rest of the board. It will live with me in my heart forever.

Brother Scott Pierce:

My sister was the most consistent person I have ever known. I knew what her reaction would be to everything that happened to her and what she would say. She was always upbeat, a good listener and storyteller, compas-sionate, and never mean, with a strong, self-deprecating sense of humor. She sincerely wanted to "do good" and did. I believe her role models were our father, an amaz-ingly able and good man, and 41's mother, Dorothy, an equally blessed lady. Between them they molded her personality into the remarkably consistent woman that we remember. With Barbara Pierce Bush, what you, ev-eryone, saw was what you got. There was nothing phony there. I admired and loved my sister very much.

Sister-in-law Janice Pierce:

Bar made me feel comfortable by introducing me as her sister (not sister-in-law). She thought about the person to whom she was talking and was generous in her remarks. If in her opinion they overstepped, she had a way of straightening them out that was to the point but not harsh. So I learned from her to try to make another feel comfortable.

She was always honest and true, no hidden agendas.

Her courage when Robin was dying was hard to imagine. I learned to move forward in adversity, smile, and get on with it!

Sister-in-law Jody Bush:

As she was fourteen years older than me, Bar had been through all the important events and relationships before I had. She was forceful, confident, funny, warm, and very smart. If you listened you had plenty to learn from her.

One lesson: **You know, Jo, we are not in a popularity contest.** This comment was made when we were talking about our relationships with our grandchildren and daughters-in-law. Why that struck me dumb is sort of pathetic—I WAS in a popularity contest. As the numbers of grandchildren increased and the chaos grew, I realized there was no way I could be other than myself and let the chips fall where they may. Bar taught me that.

Nephew Jamie Bush:

Mostly I remember a lot of one-offs. Like when I got thrown out of boarding school for drugs and was widely known as a disappointment to my parents. Aunt Bar told me on the porch of the River Club [in Kennebunkport], in essence that, once forgiven, I was forgiven. Therefore, receive it and live on as one forgiven. No more hangdog, no more acting out, just get on with it. Good message, and would have been even better if I'd truly understood it. But short and sweet. Like a lot of her rebukes (of which, not surprisingly, there were many). And she usually gave advice in short anecdotal sort of ways with a smile and a pat on the back. Would love to have seen her expressions after I'd turned away. She had enormous patience.

Niece Louisa Bush McCall:

Aunt Bar and Uncle George were incredibly generous to all of us when in Kennebunkport. They genuinely seemed pleased to let the extended cousins have the run of the place—to an extent. When [my son] Henry was fourteen, he and a friend were on the Segways, the favorite toy of all children big enough to ride but too small for cars. In their infinite teenage wisdom, they decided to ride their Segways up the wheelchair ramp, into the house, and into the hallway between the kitchen and the master bedroom. At that moment, Aunt Bar emerged from her bedroom on her walker. She looked up at Henry and said in a firm voice, **Now, Henry, are you where you are supposed to be right now?** "Sorry, Aunt Bar," he replied. The boys rotated their Segways and rolled back out of the house feeling very foolish.

My other favorite Aunt Bar story happened when [my son] William was a toddler and he HATED clothes, and especially swimwear. I asked Aunt Bar how she felt about naked children at the pool. She looked at me and said, **Louisa, if you are not old, fat, or ugly, booney wild is always permitted.**

So what did I learn from these and other frequent encounters between Aunt Bar and my often mischievous children? **Discipline but with patience.**

Niece Robin Ellis:

Did you ever get "The Look" from Aunt Bar? That stare combined with her wonderful sense of humor is something I loved, but also was a life lesson.

Aunt Bar helped me be honest and direct with people, and for that I will always be grateful.

I got that look and the words to follow plenty of times, but a number of years ago, after a swim in the pool at Walker's Point, Aunt Bar asked how the water was. Foolishly I said, "A little warm." This instantly un-leashed The Look—could I be any more ungrateful?—and the comment that I didn't have to swim in it. But the voice was more mischievous than reproachful, as she knew she had been handed material she could use for years to come. And that she did!

She made me feel comfortable enough to say prac-tically anything, and often I would come close to more unfiltered commentary about something—kids, grand-kids, Kennebunkport gossip—and my wonderful friend and cousin Doro would delight telling [my husband] Hap, "You should have heard Robin's comment today to Mom."

First cousin Debbie Stapleton:

(Taken from a letter Debbie wrote Mrs. Bush's five children after their mother died.)

What touched me deeply...was an act of kindness to a new, frazzled mom. One rainy, gray day in 1974 the doorbell rang, and I opened it to find your mother standing on the front doorstep. She asked how I was doing and came in to hear nothing but [my son] Walker wailing at the top of his lungs. I was a mess and she said, **Dearie, you need a project.** She then asked me what my favorite design would be for a backgammon board. Immediately, I thought of a childhood trip to

England and visiting Buckingham Palace. I suggested the guards and their guardhouses for the points on the board and voila, it was delivered several weeks later. It only took me fifteen years to finish...[6]

My second early memory was campaigning in New Hampshire in 1988 with [my husband] Craig, [our children] Walker, and Wendy. Bar was "meeting and greeting" in the mall when she spied Walker and Wendy, seemingly alone. I received a true BB scolding by mail and was at first hurt, since they were with campaign aides, but Craig wisely said, "Consider this a badge of honor; she is treating you as she would her own child."

Bar loved unconditionally even when she was making a point or correcting you.

First cousin Betsy Field:

It was summer in the early eighties. I, a young mother of two kids, had fled to Kennebunkport, imagining the glorious benefits of some relaxation, renewal, and, hopefully, a vacation.

But taking care of two little boys (Jay and Andrew) was an exhausting period, even on Ocean Avenue.

---

6   Mrs. Bush had sent Debbie a backgammon board needlepoint design.

Little did I know, though, that some real help might be waiting for me at Walker's Point.

We came out to see Bar and to swim and to play with cousins. But Jay's curiosity and endlessly persistent questions about almost everything prevailed. I left the pool early, undone and totally exasperated by the shortened visit.

When we returned home to Rye, New York, later that month, there was a letter waiting for me at the house. I recognized Bar's singular handwriting and the familiar image of Walker's Point on the back.

Dear Betsy,

I am so glad you came out to the Point with Jay and Andrew. I can see they are keeping you very busy, and I'll bet tired much of the time.

Please know, Dearie, that all those questions and all your answers (or not) are the real beginnings of wisdom. So, take heart and be patient.

Love to you, John, Jay and Andrew, Bar

Now there was a real Superwoman when I needed her!

It's not possible to have a chapter about family and not include her husband of more than seventy-three years. If he were alive, what would George H. W. Bush say he learned from Barbara Pierce Bush?

Perhaps this letter he wrote to her on their forty-ninth wedding anniversary provides a hint at how much he knew he had learned:

January 6, 1994

For: Barbara Pierce
From: GHWB

Will you marry me? Oops, I forgot, you did that 49 years ago today! I was very happy on that day in 1945, but I am even happier today. You have given me joy that few men know. You have made our boys into men by bawling them out and then, right away, by loving them. You have helped Doro be the sweetest greatest daughter in the whole wide world. I have climbed perhaps the highest mountain in the world, but even that cannot hold a candle to being Barbara's husband. Mum used to tell me: "Now, George, don't walk ahead." Little did she know I was only trying to keep up—keep up with Barbara Pierce from Onondaga Street in Rye, New York. I love you!

CHAPTER 2

But Friends Are Right Behind

I can still hear her voice in the back of my head. I hope it never goes away.
—Catherine Branch Plumlee, personal aide to Mrs. Bush

Mrs. Bush famously told the Wellesley graduates in 1990 that **human connections—with spouses, with children, with friends—are the most important investments you will ever make.**

Anyone blessed to call her a friend knew just how rich that investment was. Whether you were a next-door neighbor, a carpool partner, a fellow First Lady or a former president, a celebrity or someone who worked for Barbara Bush—you always knew she would be there for you.

Perhaps no one knew or understood that better than James Baker, who was George Bush's closest friend for nearly sixty years, and his second wife, Susan, who had become one of Mrs. Bush's best friends. The Bakers spent Mrs. Bush's last night on earth with the two of them, Mrs. Bush sipping a Manhattan, the two men drinking martinis. (Susan, perhaps wisely, chose water.)

And they were there at President Bush's bedside eight months later when he took his last breath.

For the men, the friendship began on a tennis court when the Bushes moved from Midland, Texas, to Houston in 1959. Together they survived political defeats and victories; the pinnacle of success, one as president and one as secretary of state; and the toughest time of anyone's life— the loss of a loved one. Secretary Baker remembers one such moment well when he was about to lose his first wife, Mary Stuart Baker, to cancer.

In early February of 1970, Barbara Bush entered Room 357 at Houston's Memorial Hospital with her husband, George, to visit my dying wife. In doing so, she taught me an enduring life lesson.

It was cold outside, as temperatures had been trending toward freezing that week as Houston was experiencing a winter cold snap. But inside, Barbara warmed the room with her love and tenderness, kind traits she displayed throughout her life. Barbara and

George were the last non-family members Mary Stuart saw before she passed away February 18. It was a classic Barbara Bush moment, supporting a good friend during her final days and bucking me up at a time when I needed it badly. Some people have viewed Barbara as tough as the West Texas hardscrabble oil patch where George got his start. But I always believed that those people misinterpreted her honesty and directness for callousness. They couldn't be further from the truth. In addition to being the gold standard of First Ladies, Barbara Bush was a wonderful human being who did whatever she could to help a friend, whether that meant speaking the truth to them—or just being there when they needed her.

Often, the pearls of wisdom she provided were through her actions and not her words.

Susan Baker:

How blessed I have been that Barbara Bush was my friend for over fifty-five years! Her warm and outgoing personality was a magnet for so many, probably because we all sensed that she really was interested in knowing us and being a friend. She taught me how to be more kind, and more supportive, even to those considered as difficult. That's not to say she was all sweetness and light! She could be formidable, and she wouldn't hesitate to tell someone "how the cow ate the cabbage" if it was called for. I'll never forget writing Bar a note in the early '80s letting her know that her kind treatment of an extremely pushy individual made me feel ashamed of myself and taught me a lesson. Her response to the students who had belittled her when she accepted the Wellesley graduation invitation taught them a great life lesson by her graciousness. Her kind responses to strangers was an inspiration as well. She replied with encouragement and thanks to hundreds, even thousands, of people with whom she corresponded but never met.

Bar was always there for those of us who needed her, as I desperately did when Jim and I moved to Washington. There were so many others who received her supportive care that made a tremendous difference. For instance, no one knew about the little boy in the neighborhood that she read to several times a week. His parents were divorcing, and Bar was worried because he was so sad. There were countless other examples of her quiet kindnesses, as well as her loving public display to AIDS patients and others.

Bar taught us volumes about who our neighbors are, and how to love them. Her tough love and firm parenting, along with 41's supportive love, has created a cohesive and loving family, children, and grands who are following in their footsteps, all committed to make this world a better place.

We asked people from all walks of Mrs. Bush's very rich life if they would share something they learned from their friend, boss, mentor.

Like Secretary Baker's story, the lesson was often learned by watching her.

But just as often, the lesson came in the form of just plain commonsense advice and memories of a special friendship.

Robert Gates:

Lessons learned from Barbara Bush:

One on humility: At a luncheon at Texas A&M University, President Bush commented, rather proudly, that an elementary school had been named for him. Barbara cracked: **Yes, by a vote of four to three.**

Maybe the category for this one is "Not even Barbara Bush is always right." I was riding with her on Marine One when she read that Donald Trump had divorced his first wife to marry a much younger woman. I learned she didn't have much patience with men who sought trophy wives when she said: **That man will never set foot again in the White House as long as I have anything to do with it.**

In the category of manners or social graces: I was doing a jigsaw puzzle with Barbara on a cruise. We were completing the puzzle and I picked up the last piece to put it in place. She fixed me with a BPB glare, and I learned immediately that when you are someone's guest, you do not get to place the last piece in the puzzle. I meekly handed it over to her.

As it turns out, a lot of lessons were learned while doing a jigsaw puzzle with Barbara Bush:

Grandson Jeb:

Never (and this was a big one!) lean over a puzzle table or touch pieces if you didn't intend to move them or know where they were going. (Ganny was an incredible puzzler.)

Norma Major:

Whenever we stayed at Walker's Point, Barbara and I would retreat to the calm of the sitting room that overlooked the ocean, where we would tackle a large jigsaw puzzle. On one occasion, soon after George had lost the 1992 election, we commiserated about the result. As Barbara shuffled through some pieces in the box, she looked up and said: **I always think of politics as a jigsaw. You spend all your time and energy trying** to put every piece in place, and then someone comes along, tears it all up, and starts all over again.

Granddaughter Lauren:

Don't hover. My grandmother was a pro puzzler and whenever we would puzzle together in Maine, she would enforce this important rule. Hovering in puzzling (and in life) means you are not productively making a move and also obstructing others from doing so. Study the puzzle and make a move when you have one to make, but in the meantime, be considerate of others.

Likewise, a lot of lessons were learned on the golf course:

Grandson Robert:

Ganny taught me the importance of watching my golf ball off the tee as a young lad. When we would play together, I would often slice my driver way off to the right and drop my head in frustration, completely taking my eye off the ball. Rather than letting me drop another, Ganny would have me find my ball to teach me the importance of keeping my head about me and my eye on the ball, even if it did not end up where I wanted it to go. She in turn taught me how to be a much more enjoyable golf partner.

Grandson Jeb:

Never, I mean never, walk or stand behind someone when they are hitting a golf ball. (Was chewed out for three holes for doing this.)

Betsy Heminway:

When playing golf, BB always warned: **Don't say "good shot" until the ball has landed.** Whenever she played golf with various people, the minute she hit the ball they always said "good shot" and it drove her crazy, as most of the time it was a lousy shot and she knew it. Trying to butter up the First Lady was never a good idea!

Like some of her family members, many friends contributed bullet points of Mrs. Bush's "dos and don'ts" of life:

David Bates:

- **Just be yourself**. She was always just that.
- **Be direct or frank with everyone**, assuming, of course, that your motives are right and you have the best interests at heart of the person you're addressing, which she always did.
- **Have self-confidence**. Be prepared and do your

best; hold your head up, look people in the eye, and speak and act with confidence.

Anita McBride:

She was a mother to all of us. But it was advice she shared just a few years ago when my family came up to Kennebunkport for a visit that I remember best. At a fun lunch, Mrs. Bush asked our son Andrew about his college search and offered this advice to him:

- **Shoot high.**
- **Don't use drugs.**
- **Don't lie.**

She added that lying ruined Richard Nixon's presidency.

Mrs. Bush's great advice was not lost on our daughter Giovanna, who just went through her own college search. Her words of wisdom and influence live on in our household.

Russell Levenson:

- **Be generous**. The president and Bar were two of the most generous people we ever encountered— they gave of their resources, their time, energy, wisdom, and good spirit. They gave to big things, and in small ways.

- **Laugh a lot**. In our eleven years of friendship, we always managed to laugh—even when in the hospital, or at times of uncertainty about health. Bar always managed to say something worthy of a smile—and she did love a good joke.
- **Pray**. We prayed together a lot, especially in the last years. We would hold hands and pray. The longer she lived, the more she prayed.

Julie Cooke:

- **Find something nice to say about someone**, even if it's a stretch. It's always better.

She taught me to be a better mother-in-law, and taught me this lesson she learned from HER mother-in-law: **When George and I were newly married, George's parents asked us to babysit for George's little brother Bucky. We did so happily. Afterward, George's mother, Dorothy, told everyone, "You know Barbara is the BEST cook!" The truth is that all I had done was make peanut butter and jelly sandwiches. You would have thought I had made a gourmet meal! That lovely, generous woman found a way to**

encourage and praise me. I never forgot her supportive words and gesture. And I tried to do the same in
our family.

Ann Brock:

- **Do something today!**

When I was interviewed to be director of scheduling
for Mrs. Bush at the White House, she told me she
wanted to do something every day. Very simple, very
direct. And she did it every day of her life. Of course
with my job, as with everyone, I do something sub-
stantive, something productive every Monday through
Friday; however, I long for rainy Saturdays or holidays
from school where I can do absolutely nothing but
binge-watch a nine-episode TV show. But deep down
I will always hear "Do something today!" and I'm off
the couch.

- **Don't complain and don't explain.**

I had messed up something with guests from Texas.
I can't remember exactly what I did or did not do but
she was not pleased, and as I was explaining what I
thought had happened, she said: **Don't complain and
don't explain.** She then hung up. Done. Hmm, she
was right. Throughout my life after that very short,

very direct phone call without a goodbye at the end of the conversation, I adopted that very same instruction. So simple, so direct, and so Barbara Bush. Even today I cannot stand it when someone rattles on about why it took them so long or gives a step-by-step reenactment of how they couldn't get something done. Ugh. Just bottom-line it. Did it get done—yes or no?

Duane Allen:

- **Don't feed Millie!!!!!!**
- **Don't brag on oneself.**

When we were houseguests in Maine, I learned that she did not like me going to the kitchen and eating a bowl of Texas-made and -sold Blue Bell ice cream between meals. I always keep Blue Bell ice cream on our tour bus, so I learned if I had a good supply, it was smart to restock her freezer with Blue Bell before we left.

Dava Guerin:

- **Have empathy for others, and never think you are too smart, too rich, or too entitled to put yourself in their shoes.**
- **Realize what is truly important in life—and not always in this order: family, faith, and friends.**

- **Listen to others and be respectful, but not afraid to speak your mind when appropriate.**
- **Use self-deprecating humor when you know others will be intimidated by your position of power.**
- **Never pay top dollar for department store lipstick when you can get the same thing at the drugstore for a fraction of the cost!**

I have seen Mrs. Bush exhibit these qualities many times over the past thirty years. Endearing, funny, and memorable, Barbara Bush's life lessons will forever be ingrained in my life. They startle me every day.

By now you likely have noticed several major themes emerging in the advice given by Mrs. Bush:

- *The importance of family and being a good parent.*
- *Be yourself. Say what is on your mind. Don't put on airs.*
- *Treat people the way you want to be treated.*
- *Be flexible.*
- *Enjoy life.*

The last point was one of her favorite themes. As her long-time chief of staff, Susan Porter Rose, said:

Each time George Bush reached out to a new professional experience, often requiring that they move again, Mrs. Bush coped with the upheaval of it with a wise admonition to herself: **You have two choices in life: You can either like your life, or you can choose not to like your life. I have chosen to like mine.**

I am not sure there is a more important life lesson.

Julie Cooke had the same thought:

She told her staff about when she learned she was moving to Texas. **One day George came home and announced with excitement, "We're moving to Odessa, Texas!" Well, my heart just fell. We had friends and family in the East and life was good. The thought of moving hit me hard. I paused a moment, took a deep breath and said I've <u>always</u> wanted to live in Odessa!**

To me, that epitomizes Barbara Bush's approach to life: Be positive, look for the good, and embrace life's opportunities.

Every once in a while, when a slight bump or challenge comes my way, I smile and say to myself, "I've always wanted to live in Odessa!!"

Barbara Bush's flexibility was a large part of her credo to "like your life." She was married to a man whom she likened to Perle Mesta, a legendary socialite and partygiver during her era. Mrs. Bush said she knew she was in trouble when President Bush invited twelve fellow Yale classmates to their first Thanksgiving as a married couple. He forgot his wife really didn't know how to cook.

Here are some "flexibility" stories:

Laurie Firestone:

My first day as social secretary with the Bushes was Inauguration Day, 1981. I met with Barbara prior to that and she said that they wanted to invite their family back to the vice president's house, at the Naval Observatory. I said fine—she then said there would be about 125, including children, and just do a menu that I thought everyone would like—yikes!!

Fortunately, everything went off beautifully. I met the whole family—children, brothers, sister, etc. It was the beginning of twelve exciting years for me—eight years at the vice president's and four years at the White House.

It was then that I realized what my job was going to be. Barbara Bush and the president had confidence in me and expected me to do the right thing! And to be flexible. (Heaven knows she was.) That bond between us lasted for the twelve years I worked for them.

They led and taught by example—always living each day to the fullest with humor and dignity!

Cathy Fenton, Laurie's deputy:

One evening, when Laurie and I had again QUICKLY pulled together an impromptu cocktail hour with members of Congress in the State Dining Room and all had gone well, we THOUGHT we were done for the evening and could begin to escort our guests to the front door for farewells when dear President Bush announced, "Oh, let's pop upstairs and see the private quarters—you all will love it!!" As POTUS began to lead guests up the Grand Staircase via the Cross Hall, I was corralling guests to follow and I glanced back and BPB was just adjacent to me and stared at me with obvious mixed feelings and said to me: **Cathy, I have been doing this for forty-four years!**

She was the quintessential good sport. They managed to achieve SO much in such a fast-paced four years of his presidency, and it was all because of their devotion to each other and appreciation for living life to its fullest every day.

Maybe her ultimate example of flexibility came on January 20, 1993, when the Bushes moved out and President and Mrs. Clinton moved in.

Everyone was getting ready to leave for the inauguration. I turned around and was standing face-to-face with Mrs. Bush. I looked at her beautiful, smiling face and promptly burst into tears. All my decorum and defenses broke down. She put her arms around me and said: **There, there, Cathy, all will be well, we are all going to have a wonderful life.** But it seemed anything but on that morning.

As I wandered slowly to the subway and home, I felt a keen sense of calm remembering this ever-kind, loving Barbara Bush. Life would be okay.

Mary Kate Cary:

The first time I met Barbara Bush, I was wearing her bathing suit. I was terrified. She was gracious.

It was June 1993, and George H. W. Bush had invited several speechwriters to Kennebunkport to work on a few post-presidential addresses. As noon approached, the president announced that we'd go for a dip in the icy Maine surf. Next thing I knew, he was handing me a bathing suit—a skirted one-piece—that belonged to his wife and announcing I had no excuse.

As we headed to the pool—the presidential plan had us stopping there to get used to the water—I spied the former First Lady with several of her Texas friends. "Ladies," called out the president. "You know my speechwriters, don't you?" Not wanting her to think I had rifled through her closet and helped myself, I said, "Pleasure to meet you, Mrs. Bush. I hope you don't mind that your husband loaned me your bathing suit."

I gulped, waiting for a legendary Barbara Bush takedown.

There was none. She simply laughed and said: **I'm so glad we had a suit for you. Have fun!** And that was the first of many lessons I was to learn from Mrs. Bush: If you want to enjoy life, you've got to be able to roll with it. She always made room for all the long-lost friends, the unexpected dinner guests, the staffers who needed bathing suits.

Along with flexibility, Mrs. Bush knew it was important to appreciate every single moment of life, a lesson she taught her friend Amy Updegrove:

A few years ago, my husband and I were invited to join a group of friends at a small dinner party. With the Bushes, there was a total of twelve of us at the table. The house, down the street in Kennebunkport, couldn't have held much more than that. It was an intimate setting with a view of the ocean.

While the president and Mrs. Bush spent their summers at Walker's Point in a house many times the size of this home and enjoyed a much more spectacular view out of their own windows, it did not stop them from appreciating the beauty of the evening. Before the dinner began, everyone was milling about and visiting. I was standing next to Barbara (as she had asked me to call her), looking out of the window at the glorious sunset beyond. **We are so lucky,** she said.

I saw this each time I was with her. I learned from her never to take anything—any moment—for granted.

Barbara had a deep appreciation for life, yet remained pragmatic about living. It wasn't that she offered advice. It was that she invited emulation. Her words and actions always showed her gratitude, her grace, her enthusiasm, her strength, and her morality.

If you knew Barbara Bush and if you had children, you likely received parenting advice at one time or another. Family was, after all, the centerpiece of her life.

Ron Kaufman:

In one of my first few weeks in the White House in 1989, my hometown paper, the *Quincy Patriot Ledger*, sent a reporter to spend a day with me. Yes, for me, it was a big deal.

As we sat in my office late that evening, he asked how did I like these "fourteen- to fifteen-hour days." To which I responded, "I love to come to work every day and hate to go home at night!"

A few days later, after the article appeared in the White House morning news clips, I ran into Mrs. Bush in the White House mess.

Read your story. Nice quote, boy genius! Let me give you some advice. Go home early today and spend some time with your family!

As always, when she gave you advice—you followed it! And home I went. A few days later, in her most grandmotherly way, she asked how things were at home. I learned firsthand, from one of the world's busiest people—it is home and family that matters most!

Tom Collamore:

I would like to share a letter I wrote to President Bush in May 2018, shortly after his wife died:

...It is particularly comforting knowing that younger Americans have been introduced to this remarkable woman and will have the chance to learn from her exemplary life...

I thought I'd remind you of one story that changed my life. In 1995, shortly after our first child was born, we learned that he had severe disabilities and medical challenges that would keep him from talking or living a regular life. [My wife] Jake left her fast-track New York City job and led the charge to ensure we left no stone uncovered and that our precious Tommy would have every opportunity to live a full life. We were soon blessed with our first of three daughters, but our focus remained on our son. Enter Mrs. Bush. She told us stories of her friends with similar challenges and how they had coped. She urged us to keep on living and be sure our daughter Pauline received as much attention as our son. And when she sensed we weren't following her good advice to a healthy degree, she encouraged you to include Jake and me on one of your Greek cruises.[7] To see the sights and enjoy the company of the two of you, your friends and family was the cover story—but we knew the subtle but very real purpose was to teach us how to leave home and get back to living a full life. It worked. We came home with a new perspective. It didn't alter our intense efforts to give our son every chance, but it gave us needed balance and ensured that we parented our daughters with the same love and attention we were giving our son. No lectures were given—just compassionate and caring concern from special friends. We were the lucky recipients of Mrs. Bush's keen understanding of parenting, family, and love.

Another common theme was Mrs. Bush's strong belief in humility:

---

7   For several years President and Mrs. Bush hosted family and friends on a cruise of the Greek islands.

David Bates:

I first met Mrs. Bush at the age of eleven in 1963 when I became a friend of Jeb's. I was at the house frequently. Mrs. Bush was a commanding presence even then. President Bush was often away on business, thus, Mrs. Bush had to do the job of two in raising the Bush kids. And a wonderful job she did. She instilled in them respect for authority, discipline, good manners (including modesty), and frugality.

Regarding the latter, I remember playing Ping-Pong with Jeb at his house, and Mrs. Bush came into the playroom with a bill from the Houston Country Club. Jeb had signed for a hamburger for lunch. Mrs. B was not pleased and let Jeb know it. Our other friends and I whose parents belonged to the club were allowed to buy lunch at the club during the summer, but the Bush children brought their lunches in brown paper bags.

Mrs. Bush was clearly a strict parent. Most of my friends and I preferred not to spend time at such parents' homes, as the atmosphere tended to be more like a schoolroom. But that was not the case with Mrs. Bush. We clearly knew we had to be on our best behavior in her presence, but we enjoyed being around her. She was always loving and interested in each of us as a person.

Ashley O'Neil:

The lesson I learned from Mrs. Bush is that you are never too important a person in this world.

She demonstrated this to me one early morning when we were slowly walking the Kennebunk beach together with Sammy, my Norwich terrier, and her two dogs, Mini and Bibi. I spotted a very large "deposit" from a very large dog in her path and said, "Watch out for that, Mrs. Bush." Instead of veering around it, she slowly stopped and dug deep to find an extra poop bag and proceeded to bend over and clean up the giant pile (while I turned my back and couldn't watch). To this day I still marvel and reflect on that moment: The former First Lady of the United States cleaned up someone else's dog poop!

The fact that she was humble didn't mean she never spoke her mind. She always spoke her mind and encouraged others to do the same. Some tidbits and observations:

John Major:

I was with George shortly before his eightieth birthday celebration, when he was trying to persuade me to join him on one of his famous parachute jumps. His offer was deeply resistible but, before I could reply, my wife, Norma, intervened—in very clear and forceful terms. "No way," she exclaimed. Barbara was clearly enjoying the exchange. **You see, George. That's why women are so sensible. We're the ones who always keep our feet on the ground.**

Another time we were staying at Walker's Point one summer, when George invited my son James—then sixteen—to come out on his boat. "It'll be great," said George. "The bluefish are biting. I'll teach you how to catch them."

We were out on the water for some time, so great things were expected. When we finally returned, Norma asked James how many they had caught. "Ummm, none," was his reply.

Barbara wasn't surprised. **If we had to live on what George caught, we would all go very hungry—and I wouldn't have to walk the dog so far each day.**

Dan Quayle:

As we all know, Barbara was always willing to give her opinion, which was always candid and truthful. When I would ask her about a person, she would always go to the bottom line—either she trusted that person or she didn't trust that person. Trust was her defining characteristic of people. And she's right. It is a lesson well learned.

Christopher Buckley:

You could learn a lot, being around Barbara Bush. She had a reputation for being direct, and boy could she be. But she was also capable of subtlety. One afternoon in Houston I had a lovely lunch with her and Mr. Bush prior to attending a matinee performance of *Frost/Nixon.* (One would have thought Mr. Bush had had enough of all that, having served as head of the GOP during Watergate. Nonetheless...) Mr. Bush and I both had a couple of Bloody Marys. I promptly fell asleep about ten minutes into act 1, with Stacey Keach and Michael Sheen onstage, about ten feet in front of us. (Mr. and Mrs. B tended to get good seats at the theater in Houston.) I compounded my combo *faux-pas* and *lèse-majesté* by starting to snore.

Rather than smack me with her handbag, Mrs. B said very quietly to Mr. B: **Christo is snoring.**

I was asleep, and yet I heard her. Such was the power of Mrs. B, that you could hear her, even through the fog of vodka. I awoke, instantly, and sat bolt upright for the rest of the show.

Jon Meacham:

I was fortunate enough to know Mrs. Bush in two senses: first, as the formidable woman who graciously extended her hospitality to this doubtlessly annoying

biographer and, second, as someone who read her immense diaries of life from 1948 forward.

And here's the important thing to know: She was the same in person and in private, in public and behind closed doors, in company and alone with her thoughts. This is a remarkable thing, for many of us—I'd venture to say *most* of us—tend, in T. S. Eliot's phrase, to prepare a face to meet the faces that we meet.

Barbara Bush had one face. Her candor—about virtually everything—was bracing and real. So was her grace and her determination, which she shared with her husband, to put others first, or at least to try to. What you saw was what you got. In the privacy of her diary, which she kept with remarkable discipline, Mrs. Bush was as honest about herself as she was about others and was endlessly *grateful*—grateful for kind words, for hospitality extended, for good fortune.

So that, among other things, is what she taught me: Be honest and be grateful. She was both. The rest of us can only try—but here's hoping we do it, because I know she's watching, and probably still keeping that diary.

Michael Dannenhauer:

One thing BPB taught me was to speak my mind— even when speaking with <u>her</u>.

I was with 41 and BPB in a European capital,

which one, I don't remember, and we were at an event where one of the speakers went on…and on…and on…and on. It might have been that I was jet-lagged, but I thought this guy would never finish. He finally did and the program continued with President Bush speaking. After the event he headed off to play golf, so I headed back to the hotel with Mrs. Bush. As we rode together, she asked me what I thought of the event—and I told her I thought the speaker was a blowhard, that he loved hearing the sound of his own voice, and that he droned on for far too long. She glanced over at me, with that BPB look, and told me how lovely she thought he was and that he was a close personal friend she hadn't seen in a while. I, of course, began to mumble out some apology for offending her—but she quickly stopped me and said I should never be afraid to give my opinion—even to her—and that she appreciated my honesty. Then we both had a good laugh about it. I think she honestly felt the same way about the speaker—old friend or not!

Once in a while Mrs. Bush would maybe engage in gossip. Okay, she loved to gossip. Her co-conspirators admit they even learned a thing or two while exchanging interesting tidbits:

Rob Portman:

Later in life, when my wife, Jane, and I would visit the Bushes in Houston or Kennebunkport, she loved good political gossip, and her questions and comments were pointed and direct. When asking about my colleagues in the House or Senate, or candidates in the news, her questions and opinions weren't about whether they were liberal or conservative, but about their character. Humility, loyalty, and teamwork impressed her more than charisma or the ability to deliver a good speech. Being around her was a reminder of the importance of practicing good character. Maybe partly because you knew you could be the next subject of her commentary, but mostly because you knew she was right about what matters most.

Peter G. Cheney:

Barbara will be remembered in part for her many spontaneous and candid utterings—often humorous and sometimes biting. On more than one occasion, she made an observation about someone when I was with her, only then to say: **George will be unhappy with me for saying that.** She would pause and continue: **But it's true!**

Barbara Bush was clearly not one to "watch her tongue." But her candor is not chiefly why she will

71

be treasured. Barbara was fueled by compassion, and like her great husband, she lived to serve others, most often those in the most challenging of circumstances. No matter how different another person's background, station in life, or perspective, Barbara valued and treated all as human peers. I will forever be grateful to have learned this most important life lesson from this remarkable woman.

Reverend Cheney's observation about how Mrs. Bush treated everyone as a peer is the perfect segue to another round of stories.

Teri Hatcher:

Mrs. Bush taught me many little things that are big things. Through her generosity toward others, I witnessed that there is truly an endless supply of it and infinite ways to make other people feel seen and heard and respected, if with nothing more than a welcoming smile or hello.

Really the way she treated people, the consistency of a combination of humor and kindness and fortitude, has always been inspiring.

She once witnessed and commented on how well-mannered my young toddler daughter was at their family dinner table. Apparently a recent young visitor who will go unnamed was rude, so by comparison, my daughter caught Mrs. Bush's eye in a positive way.

It's impossible to say how joyful I was to get the seal of approval for teaching my daughter good manners!

Gian-Carlo Peressutti:

One of the first things I realized about Mrs. Bush was that she would speak to someone she had just met with the same sense of unguarded honesty as she might to her oldest acquaintance and friend. I'll never forget traveling with her to Southern California in the late '90s. We had entered the lobby of the resort at which the former First Lady was to speak later that evening and a local Secret Service agent was escorting her to her room. As she walked down the hallway toward the elevator, Mrs. Bush paused, turned to the agent, and said: **My. Have you ever seen such ugly wallpaper in your entire life?** Being a highly trained member of an elite law enforcement organization, the agent simply pursed his lips ever so slightly and they kept walking. But the truth was, had he replied, either in agreement or even in disagreement, Barbara Bush would have welcomed the response and considered his opinion. For as much as she espoused candor herself, she appreciated it in others as well.

Of course, that unbridled honesty could certainly be

biting at times, too. At last count, Mrs. Bush "fired" me on three occasions in the four years that I worked for her husband. Whereas I was pretty certain in each instance that my termination was only temporary, there was no question that the sentiment behind it was all too real, however momentary.[8]

I doubt I'll ever have the gumption to be as constantly candid as was Barbara Bush, but I certainly have come to appreciate this characteristic in others.

Jim Appleby:

I never received an in-your-face piece of advice from Mrs. Bush, but the way in which she composed herself and interacted with others was a life lesson in itself. As a "yard lad" and as President Bush's aide, I saw her working hard to ensure every family member and friend that visited Walker's Point every summer had a wonderful experience—whether it was making sure that rooms and beds were available or that everyone had a seat at the dinner table for breakfast, lunch, or dinner—she was inclusive of everyone.

As President Bush's aide I had the unique perspective of watching firsthand the love that Mrs. Bush had for

---

8   Mrs. Bush used the term "You're fired" rather loosely, but to my knowledge never really fired anyone. At least not directly.

President Bush—and that love carried over into everything she did and everyone she interacted with. While she could be a tough lady at times, I learned from her that everyone matters—no matter where you come from, no matter what your level of education, position, background—everyone matters. It is a trait she shared with President Bush.

She also helped reinforce for me the principle of loving thy neighbor. She was constantly encouraging people to visit, whether it was a visit to Maine, Houston, or catching up in College Station or while she was traveling. Friendship was immensely important, and she worked hard to keep up with family and friends throughout the year.

Dante DeLorenzo:

On my first day of working for the Bushes, I was introduced to Mrs. Bush. Being a fifteen-year-old boy, I was obviously very nervous to meet such a wonderful lady. Knowing that I was nervous, she found a way to make me more comfortable.

She told me she read the local newspaper that morning, and knowing that I played football, she made a joke about my team not being good enough to make it into the paper.

I worked for her the next summer. And when

August came around, she started asking me about my team. She wanted to know how my team was going to be and how I was as a player. When the season started, every Saturday morning I would ask her if she needed me to do anything. And every morning she would ask me about my game, and we would talk about it for a little while. She would always get excited when I would tell her that I scored a touchdown. When Mrs. Bush and President Bush went back to Texas in the middle of October, I still had a few more games to play in my season. She asked me to send her an email every Saturday morning to let her know how the game went. She kept her word and always got back to me right away.

I admire the fact that a woman of her experience and background would be so interested in something that was such a big part of my life. She taught me you can always find common ground between people, even when they are at different stages of their lives. Mrs. Bush took the time to learn about the lives of the people who worked for her. She cared about them as people, not just employees. I learned from her that no matter who you are or where you come from, people are people, and if you care about them enough, you can always find common ground.

Gregg Petersmeyer:

In the summer of 1975, President and Mrs. Bush invited me to come spend a month with them in China, where they were living at the time. As Barbara Bush showed me around the one-floor living quarters, I stopped in front of a wooden library card catalog standing on its own legs, designed for three-by-five cards and containing twelve or sixteen drawers. I had seen them in every school or public library I ever visited, but never in a house and certainly not as a piece of home furniture. Yet there it was in the main hallway of their living quarters, right between the living room and dining room and not far from their treasured oil painting of their daughter Robin, who had died at age three.

So I asked what the file catalog held. Mrs. Bush said it was for their friends, those they sent Christmas cards to. Seeing the volume of file cards in just one drawer, I asked, "But who are all these people?" to which she replied, **Friends of ours—former neighbors, campaign supporters, people George knows from business, our mailmen.** Still trying to grasp the number of cards, I said, "So not real friends?" to which Barbara Bush replied, **No. Friends just like you!** Lesson learned. Everyone they met—from the mailman to the rich and famous, they were all "friends just like you."

As you've already seen, the staff who worked for George and Barbara Bush during their more than fifty years in public life were part employees, part friends, part family. And yes, the recipients of many lessons learned, sometimes the hard way. Here are some of their stories. I might add that they all told me she made them better, smarter, more efficient staffers.

Andrew Card:

If I ask you what you know, I do not want to know what you think.

Other variations: **I didn't ask what you think.**

Many times this and a glare would motivate fear but she taught me discipline.

There were also times when my "know" was wrong and she would repeat the "know" with sarcasm and a loving squint.

Rob Portman:

I quickly learned as a twenty-something volunteer doing advance work for then vice president Bush that "Mrs. B" was in charge. Not in charge of policy formulation or day-to-day operations, but in charge of setting the tone. That became even more evident in my later roles as a White House staffer.

She had zero tolerance for the arrogance that too often accompanies White House service and politics

78

in general. She discouraged hubris and encouraged humility, loyalty, and teamwork. Her advice, unstated but clear, was don't get too big for your britches.

Antonio Benedi:

I traveled quite a bit for the presidential and vice presidential campaign in 1979 and 1980. Once the inauguration was over, I traveled with Vice President Bush and was asked to travel also with Mrs. Bush. It seemed at the time that some advance people were a bit nervous to travel with Mrs. Bush. It wasn't anything she did; it was the mere fact that she knew more than any advance aide assigned to her.

The lessons I learned after traveling with Mrs. Bush were rather simple, if you paid attention. It was that you absolutely had to know just about every aspect of your visits. Know every name of every host you would encounter and know what they did for the visit. Another big lesson, especially overseas, was to know historic sites that you would see during a motorcade or a tour. This almost did me in when I was in the car with her on our way from the airport in Rome to the ambassador's residence, where she would meet up with the vice president. I think I can still name every landmark, fountain, and church in Rome to this day.

Taylor Blanton:

People who have spent much time with Barbara can ask each other many times, "Have you been in trouble with Barbara?" She liked to let you know if she thought you had done something wrong. Some may have resented her for doing so, but I maintain that she did it because she wanted to be everyone's mother and sincerely felt you needed to know so you would not do it again. I'm seventy-seven now and there are still times when I do or do not do something because I think that is what Barbara would have wanted. For example:

I was driving both Bushes to a campaign event in Galveston in 1964 and threw the tiniest piece of paper out the window. Barbara flew all over me for having done so, while GHWB defended me by saying, "Bar, it was just a small piece of paper." Despite his defense, I learned my lesson and for fifty-four years have never thrown anything, no matter how small, out the window again.

Some of the stories Mrs. Bush's friends shared defied being put in a category, but they were too sweet—or funny— not to share.

Several friends talked about the lesson learned on how Mrs. Bush determined the seating at all her dinner parties: She took a deck of cards and cut each card in half. Each guest then drew a half of a card—men, red; women, blue—and found its match on the table, and that's where they sat.

Here are Reba McEntire's memories of such dinners:

I was scared to death of her. I loved and respected her so much! What scared me was her bluntness. It was almost like she could read your thoughts in your mind, and that's a very scary thing. She was very wise.

The thing about cutting the playing cards in half and putting one half in a bowl and the other on the plate before dinner took place I thought was genius. And when I asked her why she did it, she said: **So when you're going home from a dinner party you and your partner have something to talk about. If you were sitting together, you already knew what each other had learned from the evening.**

So you could say Mrs. Bush taught me how to make dinner parties a lot more interesting.

Chase Untermeyer:

In the fall of 1977, I was part of an amazing group that accompanied George and Barbara Bush on their first trip back to China since they had lived there two years before. While in Beijing, we saw the famous places she had taken visitors numerous times: the Forbidden City, the Summer Palace, the Western Hills, and the Great Wall. Upon arrival at the wall, I was following the crowd toward a low-rise section off to the right when I felt a firm hand on my shoulder. It was Mrs. Bush.

That's the way everyone typically sees the Great Wall. But the real way to see it is to the left.

This was a sharply rising section—rising so sharply, in fact, there was a hand railing so visitors could pull themselves up the steep slope and brace themselves during the descent. This she and I proceeded to do, meeting only a few other hardy souls, all Chinese. When we reached the top, we were rewarded with a magnificent view as well as a feeling of accomplishment far above the mob of fellow tourists, including our colleagues on the trip.

The lesson was clear: If you follow the crowd you can do all right. But if you go the hard way you can get spectacular results.

Tim McBride:

We were a couple of weeks into my three-month trial period as Vice President Bush's personal aide when I received a call from the VP's executive assistant inviting me to join the Bushes for dinner with some friends at the VP residence a few days later. Their guests were Mr. and Mrs. Jack Valenti, who were bringing their twenty-something daughters. Mrs. Bush thought

it would be nice to have a twenty-something man at the table. I was petrified! Being the vice president's "behind-the-scenes" aide was one thing—a guest at the Bushes' dinner table was quite another! I was seated to Mrs. Bush's left. Feeling a bit like Eliza Doolittle, I mimicked everything Mrs. Bush did so as not to reveal I was a fraud. All proceeded well, until the stewards served the entree—whole Maine lobster, something I literally had never seen before. I continued to mirror Mrs. Bush as best I could, though I doubt I retrieved much of the lobster meat. I could not have been more thrilled when the dinner plates were cleared! But I will always be grateful to Barbara Bush for teaching me how to eat a whole lobster.

Mark Updegrove:

One of the things I quickly discovered during our friendship was that she didn't abide long-windedness. Who could blame her? Throughout a long life of unending public events, she had heard more than her share of those who droned on and on, intoxicated by the sound of their own voices. She once remarked of the patient husband of a talkative woman we both knew: **Seriously, he must either be deaf or a saint**.

I was reminded of her penchant for rhetorical brevity in the summer of 2016. My wife, Amy, and I were in

Kennebunkport, where I was asked to speak at a fund-raiser for the Kennebunkport Public Library. The night before, we hosted a dinner for President and Mrs. Bush and a small group at the home we rented, a delightful occasion full of easy conversation and laughter. As the evening wound down, I walked Mrs. Bush to her black Secret Service SUV.

You know, George and I are coming to your speech tomorrow night, she said as she got in the backseat.

"Yes, I know," I said. "I'm honored."

What will you be doing? she asked.

"Oh, I'll speak on presidential leadership for about forty minutes, then take ten minutes of questions," I said.

Make it thirty minutes. No questions.

The following night, I wasn't taking any chances. I spoke for twenty-nine minutes. No questions. You didn't mess with Barbara Bush.

"How was that?" I asked her afterward.

Good, she replied. Then she kissed me approvingly on the cheek.

I often think about that when I'm speaking to a group, imagining the beloved former First Lady telling me to wrap it up before I go on too long. That's one of the many things I learned from her. You should always leave with them wanting a little more—just as she did when she passed on in April of 2018. Despite her ninety-two fruitful years, she left us too soon.

Sondra Haley:

I learned early on that loyalty is a two-way street with Barbara Bush. I was, of course, loyal to her from day one, but it was the next thirty-five years that I was on the receiving end of her loyalty.

I started as an intern in the vice president's press office in 1983, eventually landing in Mrs. Bush's office in a catch-all job. There were only six of us, so we wore many hats. I had graduated from the University of Southern California Journalism School with an emphasis in public relations, so naturally any media requests, interviews, photo shoots, etc. came my way. But it was the summer of 1988, during the Bush-Quayle campaign, when Mrs. Bush changed the trajectory of my life. It became clear one of two women would be the next First Lady—Barbara Bush or Kitty Dukakis. The media interest picked up exponentially for both ladies. Overnight, Mrs. Bush needed a press secretary. The campaign descended on the vice president's residence with a list of names of competent, impressive candidates, but without interviewing a one, Mrs. Bush selected me. In the scheme of things, I had very little experience, but she wanted someone who knew her and her family. Someone who knew how she would answer an interview question or respond to a journalist. Someone she was comfortable spending a boatload of time with. Someone who was loyal.

And she was loyal to me.

So, just like that, I was thrown onto the national stage, or rather into the frying pan. I was twenty-six.

She saw my potential and my strengths. She knew I could do it before I did. Her faith in me displaced my fear of the role and the media. Her confidence in me helped me grow in my capabilities. She allowed me to learn on the job. And when I did screw up, she lifted me up instead of pulling me down. She responded with grace and humor and support. She did more than give me the opportunity of a lifetime; she helped prepare and strengthen me for a wide variety of future challenges and trials. And she gave me a brilliant start to a successful multi-year career in public affairs. Yes, she changed the entire trajectory of my life.

Lessons of loyalty come from unexpected people. Mine came from Barbara Bush.

And now the final word in this chapter goes to the young women who served as Mrs. Bush's personal aides, beginning with the 1980 presidential campaign and ending on the day she died. No one knew her better. She told them just about everything. They knew her secrets, her pet peeves, her dress size.

And except for her children and grandchildren, Barbara Bush likely gave them more advice than anyone else in her orbit.

Because it will sound like a broken record, we won't repeat what every single one of them wrote about being her aide: They loved her, they miss her, and she changed their lives forever.

Becky Brady Beach, 1978–1981:

Barbara Bush was my first boss just out of college and what a role model she was. She taught me love of family and country, and if you are blessed, to give that blessing to others. We traveled for the large part alone—no press, no staff, no advance. We became quite close and experienced the ups and downs of campaigning together. Her positive attitude, sense of humor, and wisdom were always (well, almost always) present. There wasn't a person she considered a stranger.

Kim Brady Cutler, 1981–1985:

Probably the most important lesson was to **enjoy life and learn to roll with the punches,** if life gives you lemons, make lemonade, because complaining doesn't move you forward...

She gave many speeches on volunteering and there were two stories she would tell that always hit home:

- About a person walking up the beach throwing starfish back into the sea and another person commenting that it was a waste of time, there were SO MANY starfish on the beach. The answer: "It matters to that one." Lesson: **No task is too small when it helps others.**

- About a guy complaining to God that he never wins the lottery and God's answer: "Please buy a ticket!" Lesson: **You need to get in the game to reap the rewards in life.**

Elizabeth Wise Doublet, 1985–1987:

Like so many others, I learned from her example, her perseverance, her dedication to the office of the vice presidency and the country. Her strength, both mental and physical, was inspiring and amazing to watch.

How many evenings would she have preferred to spend quietly with her husband rather than attend another reception?

On January 28, 1986, we were in a hotel holding room, about to go into the ballroom where three hundred some guests awaited her speech at a sit-down luncheon. Then suddenly the space shuttle *Challenger* exploded before our eyes on the television we were watching. We were dumbstruck and in tears. She had to go into that ballroom, onto that stage, on with the show. She soldiered through that terrible shock and delivered her speech flawlessly.

That was Barbara Bush.

Despite her incredibly busy schedule, she always made time for her family, even babysitting the grandchildren from time to time. I love the story Luci Baines Johnson told me while we were waiting for President Bush's funeral to begin. A few years ago, an event was scheduled at the LBJ Library, and First Ladies and daughters were to attend. Luci realized with horror that the event was scheduled on the day she had promised her granddaughter to attend an event at her school. She wrote to Mrs. Bush to explain that she just couldn't break the promise to her granddaughter, and to apologize for missing the event. Luci told me: "Mrs. Bush wrote me back, and in her letter she said: **If more mothers and grandmothers made the choice you have made, the world would be a better place.** I'll never forget it."

Casey Healey Killblane, 1987–1989:

Often while Mrs. Bush was standing in long receiving lines, people would make statements like: "Don't your feet hurt?" "I bet your feet hurt after standing here so long." "How can you stand in heels that long?"

Mrs. Bush pondered in the motorcade after an evening of standing. She paused, looked at me, and said: **Why would you ask that? Of course my feet hurt. Everyone's feet hurt. That is so boring.**

That resonated with me. Why focus on the things in life that everyone has to deal with, like I am so busy, I don't have time to do that, or I am so tired. I can hear her say we all have the same twenty-four hours in a day. That is so boring. Everyone chooses how to allocate those hours.

Peggy Swift White, 1989–1993:

Instead of advice, I'll share with you two important tips she shared with me:

- **When someone gives you a compliment on your outfit, just say thank you**. Don't tell them it is five or ten years old or that you borrowed it from your sister. Just acknowledge their flattering remark with a simple thank-you and move on.
- **Packing tip to avoid wrinkles: Place a clear plastic dry-cleaning bag in between each layer of clothing in your suitcase.** If you have really fancy clothes, you may want to stuff tissue in the arms/sleeves.

Nancy Huang, 1993–1994:

I think the best advice she gave me, in a somewhat indirect way, was to be myself. She was the most authentic person I knew. You didn't have to guess what she was thinking or if she liked something or not. She told you directly but in a way that was not critical but rather encouraging—so you didn't have to guess or worry about it!

She used to tell me that she preferred that I wore skirts above my knees. She said: **You have good legs, let them show!**

She never really did small talk. Every time you talked to her it was a real conversation. Even with kids, she was so real. She told you what she was thinking, how she felt, and when she asked about you, she genuinely wanted to know. That's what made working for her so easy.

Girls and women get so caught up in trying to be perfect, being afraid to disappoint, and trying to live up to standards in the workplace. Mrs. Bush received criticism for silly things like her white hair, but she never changed. She was truly authentic. She gave me the confidence to be myself.

Quincy Hicks Crawford, 1994–1998:

The Bushes entertained a lot, but the emphasis was always on making people feel at home. Entertaining didn't mean that things had to be perfect; in fact, plates, napkins, and silverware rarely matched or came in sets. It was fine to pick up fried chicken or serve soup and sandwiches—one of their favorite company meals was a taco buffet. **People don't really care what you're serving or what you have, they just like to be invited to your house.**

She was an avid gardener and a fan of flowers—showy flowers like sunflowers and hydrangea were some of her favorites. But when it came to entertaining, those didn't need to be perfect either. She once told me that all you had to do was gather a bunch of flowers from your garden, hold them together in a bunch, cut the bottoms off, and drop them in a vase. She was right, of course. They always look great and not too done.

She believed in working hard and going after your dreams but keeping things in check. One time she talked about a family member who was never happy with what she had. She had a husband who loved her, but in her eyes, he couldn't provide enough—their house should be bigger, her clothes should be more fashionable, the cars should be more expensive. She had so much but always wanted more of the things she really didn't need, and it caused problems in their marriage. **The goal is to find the balance between**

going after your dreams AND finding happiness in what you have.

Since her passing, I still seek her guidance on a variety of things. I KNOW she's out there listening.

Kara Babers Sanders, 1998–2000:

If George Bush's life reads like the great American novel, Barbara Bush's life reads like a collection of short stories, and I was privy to a story not many Americans saw—Barbara Bush the Working Woman.

When I met Mrs. Bush in 1997, she'd written a *New York Times* best-selling autobiography and was in the prime of her professional speaking years. She hustled like no other seventy-year-old woman I have ever known. Though we never talked about it, I suspected that for the first time in her adult life Mrs. Bush was earning her own money and paying her own expenses. I imagined how satisfying that must have felt.

Mrs. Bush ran her life with inspiring efficiency—a modern-day woman—and perhaps if she'd been born in a different era she might have risen to be a chief operating officer of a major company. Her mornings began well before sunrise. She read the paper, watched the morning news, and worked through often hours of daily "homework" from the office. Homework included things like reviewing professional or nonprofit speaking invitations, writing letters to friends, answering letters from the public, and reviewing speeches for upcoming engagements.

During my years with Mrs. Bush it wasn't uncommon for her to give upward of sixty speeches a year, raising millions of dollars for charities across the country. She was tireless. We were on the road a lot—but usually not on the weekends or when President Bush was home. Mrs. Bush preferred to be away only when her husband was away, guarding her time alone with her husband.

I think Mrs. Bush would tell all of us: Life is to be lived to its fullest. Our time with her was meant to be just one short story in our lives.

Brooke Sheldon, 2000–2003:

One of the greatest things she taught me was that I am not responsible for other people, their actions, or their happiness. While we need to do our part to be kind and generous with our time, people are ultimately responsible for their own choices. As long as that person is happy, it's none of our business if we agree with their decisions.

Michele Whalen Stanton, 2003–2006:

- **Being late is a sign of disrespect for the person you are meeting.**

That's what she said to me on my first day in the Houston office when I showed up late after underestimating traffic. To this day I do everything in my power to always be on time.

- **It's not "I" or "me" but "us" and "you."**

Just like President Bush, Barbara Bush was not a person who believed in talking about herself. She would tell me to count the number of times the words *I*, *my*, and *me* were used in letters—write that number down at the top of the letter—then rewrite the letter eliminating or greatly decreasing that number. Now I always refer to "my" daughters, Clare and Virginia, as "our" children.

Kristan King Nevins, 2006–2008:

Two lessons I would like to share:

My husband, Kyle, and I were married quite awhile before starting a family. Any time we visited Maine or saw the Bushes at a Barbara Bush Foundation event, they would politely ask for an update. Once we finished, she would also ask about plans to start a family. She would always encourage us to have a well-rounded "successful life" to include children. Once I had children of my own, I understood why she emphasized their additions.

Less is more. Kyle and I were sitting in a private box with the Bushes in Austin for the annual Texas A&M vs. University of Texas football game showdown. It was quite a scene—the Bushes, Texas senators Kay Bailey Hutchison and John Cornyn, Governor Rick Perry, etc. One elected official was holding court (aka being obnoxious) and sucking the life out of the room. Mrs. Bush leaned over to Kyle and me and simply said: **Less is often more.**

Amanda Aulds Sherzer, 2008–2010:

- **Don't worry about things outside your control.**

After Governor Bush pulled out of the 2016 presidential election, I wrote Mrs. Bush a letter talking about the world my children are growing up in and how I hoped they would one day face trials with as much integrity as her son. I think about her reply whenever I start worrying about the problems of the world outside my control:

March 3, 2016

Dearest Amanda,

What a nice note. Thank you. We are proud of Jeb. What a nutty world we are living in. Our only course of action is to do all we can to help people—feed and educate them—love them and set a good example for your children. Worry about those things you can change and let God take care of the rest. NOT easy, but it helps me.

Love to you and your adorable family—BPB

Hutton Hinson Higgins, 2010–2014:

Don't be a complainer. No one likes to hear about your aches and pains all the time. At age eighty-eight, Barbara Bush walked laps with her dogs and a walker at Gooch's Beach in Kennebunkport twice a day. She had terrible back pain but rarely confessed to her pain. While most of Mrs. Bush's friends were talking about their medications and ailments, she was tracking her daily steps on her Fitbit. This was her key to staying young!

Catherine Branch Plumlee, 2014–2017:

- **Be fearless.**
- **Be yourself, no matter what.**
- **Stand firm in the things you believe in, but by the same token, always keep an open mind.**

Even at age ninety-plus years old, she was still very curious. I loved how she never stopped learning, and how she listened to books on tape and needlepointed until her final days. She just kept going.

I will always be grateful to her (and President Bush) for being an all-encompassing, living, breathing example of how a successful life can be lived, and lived well. Mrs. Bush taught me the beauty of aging gracefully, with dignity and humility. And even now that she is gone, I can still hear her voice in the back of my head. I hope that voice never goes away.

Neely Brunette, 2017–2018:

She was dignified, but nothing was beneath her. My very first week as her aide, Mini—her white Maltipoo—was having bathroom issues. Mrs. Bush grabbed the carpet cleaner spray and handed me the paper towels. She was on her walker and moving very slow at this point, but you'd better believe we went around the entire house spraying and dabbing together—even though it would have taken someone else a fraction of the time. She taught me to never feel above anyone or anything.

Mrs. Bush taught me to never stop trying to find the humor in life. She aged gracefully, I think, due in part to this quality. Instead of allowing her health to define the last chapter of her life, she used her ailments to fuel her jokes. Even in pain she had me laughing in hysterics. She was prescribed Sildenafil, which was the generic name for Viagra, to help with her COPD (chronic obstructive pulmonary disease). She joked that she was going to turn into a man or get a second wind.

She taught all of us that in the end, laughter really is the best medicine.

CHAPTER 3

And Then There Were the Students

So have fun, love one another, make a difference, and make us proud.

—Barbara Bush

Barbara Bush's relationship with America's students was well documented throughout her public life. Whether she was reading to kindergartners, Skyping with a class of third graders, judging a 4-H cattle contest, tutoring a neighborhood child, or giving a commencement address—she loved them.

And they loved her.

And the older she got, the freer she became with the advice. After all, as she said in numerous speeches to students over the years:

Now, I can't give you any advice on how to be a good teacher, or a writer, or a scientist, or an actor or dancer—I especially can't give you advice on dancing—but at this point in my life, I can share with you some ideas on how to survive the inevitable ups and downs. After all, in eighty years of living, I have survived six children, seventeen grandchildren, six wars, a book by Kitty Kelley, two presidents, two governors, big Election Day wins and big Election Day losses, and sixty-one years of marriage to a husband who keeps jumping out of perfectly good airplanes. So it's just possible that along the way I've learned a thing or two.

So let's start with a story from a grade school—her Skyping friendship with the third grade of Brewer Community School in Bangor, Maine. It came about after she received a note from the teacher, Cherrie MacInnes, and one thing led to another, and suddenly she was video pals with Cherrie's class. In September 2012, she surprised Cherrie by visiting the school. "I will hold those memories in my heart for the rest of my life," Cherrie wrote in a column for the Bangor Daily News *after Mrs. Bush's death.*

Every Skype visit ended with a "little advice to live by," Cherrie wrote. She shared in her column some of the highlights:

Do something every single day to make the world better.

Work hard, read, be kind to others, and love your family.

Faith, family, and friends are the most important things in life. Be a good son or daughter, value and nourish your friends. Be a good friend, and know that God loves you, and I do, too.

If you work hard at everything you do, one of you may become the president, boy or girl.

My dream is for peace on earth, and that means no bullying. You can't have peace if you are bullying.

My dream is for every boy and girl in America to learn to read.

My dream is for families to eat together and read together, and for you to love your neighbors.

Please tell your parents not to smoke. Smoking causes cancer. It's bad for your heart and lungs. It's also bad for the people around you. And besides that, it makes you smell very bad.

Graduating to high school—Mrs. Bush loved speaking to high schoolers, especially since the invitations typically came from schools that had played a role in her own life.

She was thrilled in 2000 when her alma mater, Ashley Hall in Charleston, South Carolina, invited her to address a school assembly.

Don't worry, I'm not going to give you too much

advice. I remember an essay a young boy wrote about Socrates, a very smart man who lived in ancient Greece. He said: "Socrates was a man who went around giving advice. They poisoned him." But of course that is not going to stop me.

Don't waste this time at Ashley Hall. Study hard. There's no such thing as knowing too much. After all, do you want to grow up and be on *Who Wants to Be a Millionaire?* Of course you do!

Play hard, too. Life, after all, was meant to be fun. That doesn't mean break the rules and run wild. It just means have fun.

Be kind to everyone. There's no such thing as having too many friends, and the ones you make here will last you a lifetime.

Above all, live life with enthusiasm and gusto. There is a wonderful author named Robert Fulghum who during the years has spoken to many classrooms, from kindergarten to college age. He once made this observation:

"Ask a kindergarten class, 'How many of you can draw?' and all hands shoot up. Yes, of course we can draw—all of us. What can you draw? Anything! How about a dog eating a fire truck in a jungle? Sure! How big do you want it?

"How many of you can sing? All hands. Of course

we sing! What can you sing? Anything! What if you don't know the words? No problem, we make them up. Let's sing! Now? Why not!

"Do you like to act in plays? Yes! Do you play musical instruments? Yes! Do you write poetry? Yes! Can you read and write and count? Yes! We're learning that stuff now.

"Their answer is Yes! over and over again. The children are confident in spirit, infinite in resources, and eager to learn. Everything is still possible.

"Try those same questions on a college audience. A small percentage of the students will raise their hands when asked if they draw or dance or sing or paint or act or play an instrument. Not infrequently, those who do raise their hands will want to qualify their response with limitations: 'I only play piano, I only draw horses, only dance to rock and roll, only sing in the shower.'

"When asked why the limitations, college students answer that they do not have talent, are not majoring in the subject, or have not done any of these things since about third grade. You can imagine the response to the same questions asked of an older audience. The answer: No, none of the above.

"What went wrong between kindergarten and college?

"What happened to YES! Of course I can!"

And that's exactly what I hope your motto will be, for your whole life, "Yes, of course I can!"

In 2002 she spoke to the graduating seniors of the Kinkaid School in Houston, the alma mater of several of her children and grandchildren. Here are some excerpts:

Learn not to take life too seriously or things too personally. Learn to laugh with others—not at them, but with them—and at yourself. Let me give you a little example: Last spring, after I gave a graduation speech at Texas A&M University, I received a letter from a woman in the audience. She thought I would be amused to learn that when she got home with her granddaughter, the little girl excitedly told her mother that she had just heard the mother of the president of the United States speak. "Imagine," the child said. "I saw George Washington's mother."

A sense of humor helps.

It's also important that you believe in something larger than yourself, get involved in your new community. Try to help those who are less fortunate. One of the smartest people I know, my husband, once said, "Any definition of a successful life must include service to others." He has spent his life proving that to be true. Getting good grades and having a successful career are important, but so are being a good friend, and a good and generous neighbor.

Whatever you do, don't forget to dream. Many of you will change your mind a hundred times about what you want to be when you get out of college—and that's the way it should be. Just don't ever say: "I can't do that." What if Michael Jordan had said that when he was cut from his high school basketball team? Or Louisa May Alcott, author of *Little Women*, had said that when her family told her that she would never ever be able to make a living by writing? Or Walt Disney had said that when he was fired by a newspaper editor for LACK OF IDEAS? They all said, "YES, I CAN," and then they did.

Now go out and make us all proud and make something of yourself!

And then there was her biggest audience—college students.

Throughout her public life, Mrs. Bush was a tireless commencement speaker, accepting as many invitations as she could squeeze into her spring schedule. Likewise, in the fall, she often would give convocations, giving her a chance to speak to students at the beginning and the end of their school year.

Whether it was a community college or one of the largest campuses in the United States, her message was the same:

Make something of yourself. Cherish your relationships. Give back.

You also will notice that some years, there was something very specific on her mind, which helped frame her message to students.

Here are some excerpts from a few college addresses over the years:

Bennett College Commencement, Greensboro, North Carolina, May 1989

Now, it's customary for commencement speakers to give advice. Since I'm a mother of five and a grandmother of eleven you might not be too surprised to know that I—like your mother—gave advice to my gang. Advice like:

Clean your plate.

Honey, don't put that in your ear.

Don't cross your eyes; they'll freeze that way!

Don't put that in your mouth; you don't know where it's been!!

I do think there's a lot we can learn from our childhood...there's a book on the best-seller list by Robert Fulghum called *All I Really Need to Know I Learned in Kindergarten*. Some of my favorites:

"Play fair.

"Share everything.

"Wash your hands before you eat.

"Put things back where they belong.

"Don't hit people.

"Don't take things that aren't yours.

"Say you're sorry when you hurt somebody.

"Clean up your own mess.

"Warm cookies and milk are good for you."

Now, these guides for living aren't bad guides...

I hope you will remember the abiding principles and values we learned when we were young and that have been encouraged, reinforced, and nurtured here at Bennett College. I hope you will say:

I want to be fair.

I want to share.

It can be done.

And I want to help you.

Smith College[9] Convocation, Northampton, Massachusetts, September 1989

I'm not a great believer in human perfection, but I am a great believer in human effort. The world is changing very fast, and I don't think any of us has

---

9   Barbara Bush dropped out of Smith College halfway through her sophomore year after her engagement to George Bush. Smith awarded her an honorary degree during this visit, which she called a thrill of a lifetime.

quite caught up with it or learned how to live in it altogether comfortably. But what seems to matter is how genuinely we try... We all live life in one of two ways: We either do our best with what we are given, or we put in a half-hearted effort.

There's an old saying that "luck is when preparation meets opportunity." And I think that is the way we have to live: preparing yourself every day to meet the next opportunity...

These are the things life so far has taught me:

Attitude is 90 percent of reality, and attitude is choice.

Like what you do.

Serve others. You will always get back more than you give.

Laugh early and often, at yourself and with others.

St. Louis University, St. Louis, Missouri, May 1990

Don't worry if the future appears uncharted. You need not—cannot—have a game plan for life.

Decisions are not irrevocable. Choices do come back.

...As you set sail, I hope that many of you will consider three special opportunities. The first is to believe in something larger than yourself, to get involved in some of the big ideas of your time.

...The second opportunity is the opportunity to have fun...life is supposed to be fun!

...And the third opportunity is the most fun of all! The opportunity to be a successful parent...as important as your obligation as a graduate student or future doctor or lawyer or business leader may be—you are a human being first! A husband or a wife first; a father or mother first; a son or a daughter first; a friend first.

How sad it would be to fail at one of these positions, whatever your success in your career!

Pueblo Community College Commencement, Pueblo, Colorado, May 1991

I guess I can't resist giving you a little advice—after all, that is my job, as your commencement speaker.

First, I encourage you to always cherish your relationships with family and friends...

I also would like for you to think about your relationships in a broader sense. The way you feel about and interact with people beyond your loved ones, beyond the people you know here in Pueblo, and the friends you have made so far in life. I'm talking about the great need for better tolerance in our society.

Real tolerance is an ideal our country has strived for since its beginning. America was, after all, founded as a haven of tolerance for people of all kinds.

Certainly we've made progress, but we still have such a long way to go...

To be different. That is what life in America is about, after all.

...It can be difficult to be different in our society. It is too easy to be intolerant.

...Tolerance is much more than just respecting people of a different race. It is a constant stream of little acts in our daily lives, big and small choices we face every day in the way we think about, and talk about, and deal with other human beings.

It's about respecting people who have a physical or mental handicap, people who grew up different from the way you did, people who speak a different language, or practice a different religion, people who are fatter or thinner or older or younger.

...We have a proud legacy of freedom and independent thought. But we can be better. You can help us be better.

University of Michigan Commencement, Ann Arbor, Michigan, May 1991

We all should be alarmed at the rise of intolerance in our land, and by the growing tendency to use intimidation rather than reason in settling disputes. Neighbors who disagree no longer settle matters over a cup of coffee. They hire lawyers and go to court. Political extremists roam the land, setting citizens against one another on the basis of their class or race.

Such bullying is outrageous, and not worthy of a great nation grounded in the values of tolerance and respect. Let us fight back against the boring politics of division and derision. Let's trust our friends and colleagues to respond to reason.

…We must conquer the temptation to assigning bad motives to people who disagree with or who are different from us!

…We must build a society in which people can join in common causes without having to surrender their identities.

You can lead the way. Share your thoughts and experiences; your hopes and frustrations; defend others' right to speak. If harmony is our goal, let's pursue harmony.

Columbia College Commencement, Columbia, South Carolina, April 2005

Why on earth did you invite this almost eighty-year-old grandmother of seventeen to give your commencement speech?

…Just in case you think I am hopelessly stuck

in the twentieth century, I do want you to know my BlackBerry is in my purse and I can google with the best of you.

... My first real advice to each of you is to remind you that none of us are the same, none of us are perfect. But it's our cracks and flaws that make our lives together so very interesting. I know that Columbia College has a big emphasis on building character, which includes learning to respect and celebrate the differences in all of us. Please do not forget to take that lesson with you when you leave here. If we can all learn to respect each other more, I truly feel many of the other problems we face could be solved.

... Whether you realize this or not, your class has already proved itself to be strong and resilient. Just a few months after you started college, this country suffered one of the worst tragedies of our history—9/11. We all felt then the world was coming to an end, at least the world as we knew it. And yet, here you are today, ready to go out and make something of yourselves. You didn't give in to fear or despair, and I applaud all of you for that. You obviously chose your class motto well: "When the water gets too rough, keep on swimming."

How you approach life will make a huge difference.

Somebody once said there are two kinds of people in the world. Those who wake up in the morning and say, "Good morning, Lord." Or those who wake up in the morning and say, "Good Lord, it's morning." Make sure you are the former and not the latter!

We will end with what has become one of the most celebrated commencement addresses of all time.

On June 1, 1990, Mrs. Bush addressed the graduates at Wellesley College, an all-girls school outside Boston. Her message was very much the same one she had been delivering on campuses all over the country that spring, with one major difference: Some of the students were not very welcoming.

Earlier, when Wellesley announced the First Lady would be the commencement speaker, 150 of the 600 students signed a petition protesting her selection. According to some of the petitioners, "Barbara Bush has gained recognition through the achievements of her husband... Wellesley teaches us that we will be rewarded on the basis of our own merit, not on that of a spouse."

Mrs. Bush admitted years later the protest hurt her feelings, and she considered canceling. She actually had a perfect excuse: Long after the invitation had been accepted, the White House scheduled a summit meeting between President Bush and President Mikhail Gorbachev, in

Washington. Mrs. Bush could always claim she needed to stay home and entertain Raisa Gorbachev.

But she was not about to become a quitter at this stage in her life. So instead, she invited Raisa to go with her.

And as they say, the rest is history. The students gave her a rousing standing ovation. Here is the speech in its entirety. And yes, you've heard some of this before.

Thank you, President Keohane, Mrs. Gorbachev, trustees, faculty, parents, Julie Porter, Christine Bicknell, and the class of 1990. I am thrilled to be with you today, and very excited, as I know you must all be, that Mrs. Gorbachev could join us.

More than ten years ago when I was invited here to talk about our experiences in the People's Republic of China, I was struck by both the natural beauty of your campus and the spirit of this place.

Wellesley, you see, is not just a place, but an idea, an experiment in excellence in which diversity is not just tolerated but is embraced.

The essence of this spirit was captured in a moving speech about tolerance given last year by the student body president of one of your sister colleges. She related the story by Robert Fulghum about a young pastor who, finding himself in charge of some very energetic children, hit upon a game called Giants, Wizards, and Dwarfs.

"You have to decide now," the pastor instructed the children, "which you are...a giant, a wizard, or a dwarf." At that, a small girl tugging on his pant leg asked, "But where do the mermaids stand?"

The pastor told her there are no mermaids. "Oh yes there are," she said. "I am a mermaid."

This little girl knew what she was and she was not about to give up on either her identity or the game. She intended to take her place wherever mermaids fit into the scheme of things. Where do the mermaids stand, all those who are different, those who do not fit the boxes and the pigeonholes? "Answer that question," wrote Fulghum, "and you can build a school, a nation, or a whole world on it."

As that very wise young woman said, "Diversity, like anything worth having, requires **effort**." Effort to learn about and respect difference, to be compassionate with one another, to cherish our own identity and to accept unconditionally the same in all others.

You should all be very proud that this is the Wellesley spirit. Now, I know your first choice for today was Alice Walker, known for *The Color Purple*. Instead you got me—known for the color of my hair! Of course, Alice Walker's book has a special resonance here. At Wellesley, each class is known by

a special color, and for four years the class of '90 has worn the color purple. Today you meet on Severance Green to say goodbye to all that; to begin a new and very personal journey; a search for your own true colors.

In the world that awaits you beyond the shores of Lake Waban, no one can say what your true colors will be. But this I know: You have a first-class education from a first-class school. And so you need not, probably cannot, live a "paint-by-numbers" life. Decisions are not irrevocable. Choices do come back. As you set off from Wellesley, I hope that many of you consider making three very special choices.

The first is to believe in something larger than yourself, to get involved in some of the big ideas of your time. I chose literacy because I honestly believe that if more people could read, write, and comprehend, we would be that much closer to solving so many of the problems plaguing our society.

Early on I made another choice which I hope you will make as well. Whether you are talking about education, career, or service, you are talking about life, and life must have joy. It's supposed to be fun!

One of the reasons I made the most important

decision of my life—to marry George Bush—is because he made me laugh. It's true, sometimes we've laughed through our tears, but that shared laughter has been one of our strongest bonds. Find the joy in life, because as Ferris Bueller said on his day off, "Life moves pretty fast. Ya don't stop and look around once in a while, ya gonna miss it!"

The third choice that must not be missed is to cherish your human connection: your relationships with friends and family. For several years, you've had impressed upon you the importance to your career of dedication and hard work. This is true, but as important as your obligations as a doctor, lawyer, or business leader will be, you are a human being first and those human connections—with spouses, with children, with friends—are the most important investments you will ever make.

At the end of your life, you will never regret not having passed one more test, not winning one more verdict, or not closing one more deal. You will regret time not spent with a husband, a friend, a child, or a parent.

We are in a transitional period right now, fascinating and exhilarating times, learning to adjust to the changes and the choices we—men and women—are facing. I remember what a friend said, on hearing her husband lament to his buddies that he had to baby-sit. Quickly setting him straight, my friend told her husband that when it's your own kids, it's not called babysitting!

Maybe we should adjust faster, maybe slower. But whatever the era, whatever the times, one thing will never change: Fathers and mothers, if you have children, they must come first. Your success as a family, our success as a society, depends not on what happens in the White House, but on what happens inside your house.

For over fifty years, it was said that the winner of Wellesley's Annual Hoop Race would be the first to get married. Now they say the winner will be the first to become a CEO. Both of these stereotypes show too little tolerance for those who want to know where the mermaids stand. So I offer you today a new legend: The winner of the hoop race will be the first to realize her dream; not society's dream, her own personal dream. And who knows? Somewhere out in this audience may even be someone who will one day follow in my footsteps and preside over the White House as the president's spouse. I wish him well!

The controversy ends here. But our conversation is only beginning. And a worthwhile conversation it is. So as you leave Wellesley today, take with you deep thanks for the courtesy and honor you have shared with Mrs. Gorbachev and me. Thank you. God bless you. And may your future be worthy of your dreams.

CHAPTER 4

What She Taught the Rest of Us

It's important we each make a commitment
to our communities, to ideas and causes that
are bigger than ourselves.

—Barbara Bush

*Through actions and through words, you could say Barbara
Bush left behind for the rest of us a road map on how to
live a successful life.*

*Above all else, she was a doer. She not only talked about
what needed fixing, she went about trying to fix it.*

*She told her staff on her first day as First Lady that she
wanted to do something every day to make a difference—
either visit a program, host a reception, attend an event, or
talk to the media.*

You could say she started with a bang.

Just two months after moving into the White House, Barbara Bush made one of her first major public events a visit to a place in Washington, DC, called Grandma's House, a residential facility for children with HIV/AIDS.

But it was a hug seen around the world that sent a most powerful message.

The founders of Grandma's House wrote this piece for the Washington Post *shortly after Mrs. Bush died, reflecting on the enormity of what she accomplished with that visit.*

"Barbara Bush visited our facility for children with HIV/AIDS.

It was unforgettable."

by Debbie Tate and Joan McCarley

People often ask whether the famous picture of Barbara Bush cuddling one of the babies at our care home for children with HIV/AIDS was staged by White House photographers or handlers. It was not. It was a caring grandmother's genuine instinct to comfort and soothe a sick baby.

In 1989, as Bush toured our facility—known as Grandma's House—we entered the room of little Donovan, who, in rapidly failing health and frailty, began to whimper in his crib. As we lifted Donovan, Bush turned and gave us that trademark look of confidence and said, **Debbie and Joan, you're providing great care and services, but give me that baby. You don't know what you are doing!**

She was masterful, placing the baby over her shoulder and closely caressing him. He immediately calmed.

It's not every day that you receive a call from the White House requesting a visit from the First Lady. Sure enough, it was a visit we will never forget.

During the 1980s, an HIV/AIDS diagnosis was widely considered a death sentence—a stigmatized scarlet letter that ostracized victims and polarized friends, families, and communities worldwide. Hundreds of children, including prenatally drug-exposed and HIV-infected infants, were abandoned to hospital wards because of the fear of transmission through tears, hugs, or any touch of human tenderness. That is why we founded Grandma's House.

Sadly, out of that fear, along with discrimination and a lack of knowledge, many saw the children as "untouchables." Every form of discrimination was in practice; landlords refused to rent to us. And when the District's Child and Family Services Agency and Department of Housing and Community Development helped us purchase homes for the children's care, we couldn't disclose the address or nature of the homes out of fear for the children's well-being. As word leaked out about Grandma's House, even the telephone installer was reluctant to provide service.

You can imagine what a shock it was for our neighborhood to see a motorcade, backed by the full force of the Secret Service, swoop onto our tiny urban street in the heart of Washington. As Bush exited the limo, escorted by the Secret Service agents, you could hear neighbors and locals gasping, "Is that Barbara Bush?"

In a matter of minutes, she entered the home with a personality as big, beautiful, and commanding as her trademark silver hair. She greeted us as if she had always known us, saying, **Thank you for inviting me into your home. George and I want to thank you for what you are doing for the children.**

Just like that, no pretenses or airs—genuinely and motherly. She shared our love regarding the importance of children and grandchildren. She then proceeded into the playroom and insisted on sitting on the floor with the children.

It was there, on the floor, that she signaled to the world that regardless of health status—including HIV/AIDS—everyone deserves love and care.

And it wasn't just children. The White House had approved of our request to invite a group of men living with HIV/AIDS to meet the First Lady. After seeing the love Bush exuded holding a baby, one of the men asked: "Mrs. Bush, I am a man living with AIDS. Will you give me a hug?" Sure enough, she reached out and hugged him without hesitation.

Looking back at that time, despite being the First Lady and a woman of significant wealth, she was a risk-taker and a change agent, unafraid to utilize her considerable influence to change attitudes. At the height of the HIV/AIDS crisis, she singlehandedly educated the world, saying that it is okay to support places such as Grandma's House.

Sadly, not long after her visit, the beautiful chubby-cheeked baby she comforted to sleep died because of AIDS-related complications. But his living wasn't in vain. Thanks to the spotlight Bush afforded us, we became an international model for

24-hour residential care for HIV-infected infants and children. Moreover, her influence resulted in a visit from Princess Diana—equally awing. Bush and Princess Diana also helped raise funds for our organization, enabling Grandma's House to open other homes for needy children. A picture of Bush still hangs in our first Grandma's House.

With much affection and love, we are eternally grateful and cherish a life well-lived and shared with others. As the Bush family lays her to rest, we hope everyone remembers her as the embodiment of a true grandmother.

Mrs. Bush found other ways during the next few years to give support to both the gay and the HIV/AIDS communities. In 1990, she flew to Indianapolis to attend the funeral of teenager Ryan White, who died from AIDS.

Also in 1990, Paulette Goodman, executive director of PFLAG (Parents and Friends of Lesbians and Gays), wrote to the First Lady asking for Mrs. Bush's support. She wrote, "We who have lifted the veil of ignorance... know that our gay and lesbian children are fine, responsible, contributing members of our community. They deserve our love and support... full human and civil rights, and the respect accorded all citizens."

Mrs. Bush wrote back, thanking Mrs. Goodman for her letter and saying that she sounded like a **caring parent and a compassionate citizen…We cannot tolerate discrimination against any individuals or groups in our country. Such treatment always brings with it pain and perpetuates intolerance.**

The letter was leaked to the Associated Press, setting off a firestorm among social conservatives. From a New York Times *editorial in June 1990: "Barbara Bush, in short, has responded with compassion and decency to a matter affecting millions of American families. Unlike those who now attack her, she knows what true family values are all about."*

Occasionally Mrs. Bush would read something in the morning paper that would catapult her into immediate action. As the holiday season approached in 1990, she was appalled to read that numerous shopping malls were deciding that Salvation Army bell-ringers were "disruptive," and so were removing them from mall premises.

Mrs. Bush tells the story best in this diary entry:

December 5—I went to Mazza Gallerie in Washington to shop, but more to make a statement about the Salvation Army. I read in the paper that many malls across the country had banned the bell-ringers. Who can think of Christmas without the Salvation

Army bell-ringers? So we let the press know that I was going shopping at the Mazza Gallerie because they permitted the Army to stand outside with their pots and bells. I dropped $11 in the pot with the press watching. The response was immediate and good. Georgetown Mall immediately permitted them in.

When she died, the Houston-area Salvation Army newsletter gave Mrs. Bush credit for "single-handedly saving the Army's red kettle campaign."

Where did Barbara Bush find the wisdom, courage, and confidence to both dispense simple advice and give life lessons?

If she were here, she likely would say, "From George Bush." She always called him her example and inspiration.

But undoubtedly, her own life experiences had taught her a great deal about how to live life with patience, flexibility, and courage.

As a child, she did not get along with her mother, who often compared her to her thinner, prettier sister.

At age nineteen, before she ever walked down the aisle with the love of her life, he was shot down in the Pacific.

At age twenty-three, Barbara moved with her husband and her firstborn to the windswept plains of Odessa, Texas, where President Bush was to get his start in the oil business. Their first home was a duplex where they shared a bathroom with a mother-daughter prostitute team. They were a long way from Greenwich, Connecticut, and Rye, New York.

When Barbara Bush was twenty-eight, they lost three-year-old Robin to leukemia.

And then there was the whirlwind of their life, which took them from their families and roots on the East Coast to Texas, to California, back to Texas, to Washington, to New York City, back to Washington, to China, back to Washington, back to Texas, back to Washington, and then back to Texas for good. In the first fifty years of their marriage, George and Barbara Bush had lived in thirty different houses in seventeen different cities.

Mrs. Bush liked to joke that she "broke a few pieces of china" along the way.

As the wife of the vice president, she at least got to live in the same house for eight years. Not that they were home much. George Bush was perhaps the most traveled vice president in history, covering an estimated one million miles in eight years. And almost everywhere he went, Barbara Bush went with him.

She loved telling stories about her travels and the people they met: She compared Imelda Marcos to Marie Antoinette; felt that Nicolae Ceauşescu of Romania was a truly evil man; and fell in love with Margaret Thatcher's husband, Denis.

She would be the first to tell you that she often learned how to be a diplomat's wife the hard way—by trial and error.

She wrote this in her diary in April of 1982:

During a visit to Japan, George and I had lunch at the Imperial Palace with Emperor Hirohito...During that most memorable lunch I sat next to the Emperor and found the conversation pretty heavy sledding...He had a yes or no for everything with an occasional "thank you" thrown in. We were sitting in the glorious relatively new palace, so desperate for something to talk about, I said that new palace was lovely.

"Thank you," he answered.

Then I tried, "Is it new?"

"Yes"

Finally I tried: "Was the old palace just so old that it was falling down?"

He turned with a charming smile on his face and said, "No, I'm afraid that you bombed it."

I turned to my partner on the left.

A few years later, during the 1984 reelection campaign for Reagan–Bush, Mrs. Bush got into some media hot water when she was quoted as calling the Democratic vice presidential candidate, New York congresswoman Geraldine Ferraro, something that "rhymes with rich." She would write later that she never really lived down that faux pas, and her children called her the family "Poet Laureate" for years.

So maybe it should not be a surprise that by the time she became First Lady in 1989, life had taught Mrs. Bush a great deal about how to handle just about any situation that came her way, and that she was more than ready to share what she had learned with the world.

Her mission, as we've already seen, often came straight out of the newspaper headlines. When Saddam Hussein invaded Kuwait in August 1990, and when her husband announced, "This will not stand," the country spent the next few months bracing for a war that would be called "Desert Storm." Mrs. Bush told her staff that she would like to start visiting military bases from which troops had been deployed to the Middle East. She wanted to talk to the families.

In February and March of 1991, she visited eight bases and hugged thousands of spouses, children, mothers, and fathers.

Here are excerpts from a speech she gave at Fort Campbell, Kentucky, on February 22, 1991:

It's great being here with the 101st Airborne— 28,000 strong deployed…

Being here today with all of you is like staying close to family when we're sharing a great worry. And believe me, you are family. George wants you to know you are in his thoughts today and every day.

…You, the families, are in our hearts every bit as much as our men and women in the military. You are everything America stands for—courage, compassion, commitment, and spirit.

You are doing the very best you can. And that's the best possible thing you can do for your loved ones in the Gulf—keep life at home on an even keel.

…You make sure dentist appointments are kept; mortgage payments are made; homework gets done; and Little League games get watched.

I love the story about the woman who called a good friend of hers to see how she was. "I'm terrible. I feel awful," the friend said. "The children are home from school. The laundry's piled high, the dishes are dirty, and I've got the worst headache."

The caller quickly said, "You take an aspirin and climb into bed. I'll be right over, do the dishes, start the laundry, and take the children to the park. By the way, Sam's all right, isn't he?"

"Sam, who's Sam?" came the answer

"Sam, your husband," said the caller.

"My husband's name isn't Sam," said the poor woman.

"Oh dear. I've dialed the wrong number."

There was a long pause, and then a little sad voice said, "Does that mean you are not coming over?"

This story says a lot about how we need each other at times like this. I hope you all are using the wonderful family support programs here on the post...I hope you will keep reaching out to each other.

Mrs. Bush made "family" the theme of one of her last major speeches as First Lady, given at the Republican convention on August 19, 1992.

We've met heroic single mothers and fathers who have told us how hard it is to raise children when they are doing it alone.

We've talked to grandparents who thought their child-raising days were over, but now are raising their grandchildren because their children can't.

We've visited literacy classes where courageous parents were learning to read and continue their education so they could seek a better life for their families.

...We've met so many different families. And yet, they are really not so different...The parents we've met are determined to teach their children integrity, strength, responsibility, courage, sharing, love of God, and pride in being an American.

...Where will our country find leaders with integrity, courage, strength in ten, twenty, thirty years? The answer is that you are teaching them,

loving them, and raising them right now. God bless you for it!

After President Bush lost his reelection bid in 1992 to Bill Clinton, Mrs. Bush continued her crusade for the causes that meant a great deal to her. But she and her husband also both embarked on the speaking circuit, which President Bush jokingly called "white-collar crime."

Mrs. Bush was thrilled to actually get paid to do something she had been doing for free for years—giving speeches. And with giving speeches came giving out advice. Here are some excerpts, this one given to the Pennsylvania Bankers Association meeting at Disney World, May 20, 1997.

Another topic I wanted to mention, the importance of family. Unfortunately, the family IS going through a rough time in America these days. We only have to listen to the news, read the newspapers, or sometimes just look around us to see that too many families are struggling.

Instead of accepting blame, we tend to blame the government, because of certain laws that have been passed or not passed; or because of what we watch on television, the movies we attend, or the music we listen to.

We also expect others to take responsibility for our children, especially our schools. We expect teachers

to be church, parents, psychiatrists, and oh, yes, to teach our children, too.

Just a few weeks ago even *Newsweek* magazine's cover story was about this very issue, that many parents are not spending enough time with their children these days, and they were fooling themselves by thinking quality time could take the place of quantity. "It's not that sitters do a bad job, but sitters don't raise kids. Parents do," said the article. It went on to point out that this was not a women's issue, but a "family" issue, that it was crucial the fathers as well as mothers make more time for their children.

…Our children <u>MUST</u> come first. Of course, there are days when this is easier said than done. Even I can still remember how difficult it can be to have children in the house, when your days seem like an endless marathon of carpools, unmade beds, and the most asked question in America, "What's for dinner?" It can be even more difficult today, especially in homes where both the mother and father have careers and work long hours. There never seems to be enough time for anything, including the children. Those of you who are parents probably don't need *Newsweek* magazine to tell you that.

…My advice to parents who are having those

kinds of days is to forget the dishes and laundry and unmade beds and try to remember your most important job as parents: The home is our children's first school and we are their first teachers. We need to provide a strong home base and give our children love, support, and security. We also need to teach them the importance of developing character—and character does count! Character is about telling the truth, knowing the difference between right and wrong, tolerance and intolerance, and having the moral fiber to pick the right way.

…As parents, it's our job to give our children the right road map to life; to establish early on traits that will help them develop character. Good behavior and attitude can help, but without good character, they simply become cosmetic.

For a number of years, President and Mrs. Bush spoke at a series of motivational events hosted by their friend Peter Lowe. This excerpt is from the speech Mrs. Bush gave in Philadelphia on September 14, 2000.

I know there are many wonderful examples here today of the kind of caring and commitment I'm talking about. I bet if we asked for a show of hands, we'd see school board members, Little League coaches, hospital volunteers, and PTA presidents.

I also know that being a volunteer and getting involved in community activities can be very frustrating at times. It can be difficult to raise the money you need, or to get your message across, or to accomplish your goal. Sometimes you just get plain tired. It's easier to stay home and watch TV, locking your front door as protection from the outside world.

There are days when all of us think to ourselves, "What difference can I really make?" Whenever I think about the fact that ninety million Americans have trouble with reading and writing, I feel overwhelmed and discouraged.

My best advice is not to give up, to persevere.

I love the story about the missionary who was sitting in a small corner restaurant reading a letter delivered from home. As she opened the letter, a crisp, new twenty-dollar bill caught her attention. Needless to say, she was pleasantly surprised, but as she read the letter, her eyes were distracted by the movement of a raggedly dressed man on the sidewalk leaning against a light post in front of the building. She couldn't get his peculiar condition and stature off her mind. Thinking that he might have a greater financial need, she slipped the bill into an envelope on which she quickly penned

"PERSEVERE." Leaving the restaurant, she non-chalantly dropped the envelope at the stranger's feet.

Turning slowly, he picked it up, read it, watched the woman walk away, and smiled as he tipped his hat and went on his way.

The next day, walking down the street, she felt a tap on her shoulder. She found the same shabbily dressed man smiling as he handed her a roll of bills. When she asked what they were for, he replied: "That's the money you won, lady.

"Persevere paid five to one."

Now—I cannot guarantee the monetary proceeds for everyone, but after fifty-five years of married life—that's six children, fourteen grandchildren, four wars, three dress sizes, two governors, and two para-chute jumps—I've found the longer you persevere, the richer your blessings become.

Another speakers series in which Mrs. Bush participated was the Boise Office Solutions' POWER events, specifically for their women employees. This is an excerpt from a talk she gave in Denver on October 20, 2002.

Now that I've talked about our family so much that you must be fearful I'll bring out our family slides, don't worry. What I'd really like to do today is share some of the things I think I've learned in life. You could call them "pearls of wisdom."

Number 1: There's always something to be thankful for if you take time to look for it.

Unfortunately, it seems to me that especially in these uncertain times, people are always looking for the bad and never the good. Sometimes, it's easy to do that, especially when dealing with very scary issues such as the sniper that terrorized the Washington area and really all of us the last few weeks.

But that's when it becomes even more important to look for the good. Just the other day I heard someone complaining how much everything cost and they couldn't afford a thing. Their friend answered, "Living on earth is expensive but it does include a free trip around the sun every single year."

There are very few situations—no matter how sad or tragic—where most of us can't find something to be grateful for—for friends and family; for our country; for our faith. It's such a waste of energy to dwell on the bad and not rejoice in the good.

Number 2: I read the saddest thing the other day. "Most of us go to our grave with our music still inside of us."

Please don't let that happen to you. Too many of us live life too hesitantly—we're afraid to speak up at a meeting; to raise our hand and volunteer to take on a project; to ask a girl or a boy out on a date; to go someplace we've always wanted to see; or yes, sing or dance or paint a picture or write a poem. Quit making excuses and get involved. And while you're at it, have some fun. And here's a little hint: No one will notice or care if you're good at any of these things. They'll just be thrilled you're enjoying life.

Which leads me to Advice Number 3: Don't give up on your dreams or your goals. Too many of us are guilty of calling it quits too early. Make sure you're not one of them.

Advice Number 4: Never ask someone seventy years or older how they feel. Just the other day I went into a store and a woman said to me, "You look great. How do you feel?" I told her I feel great but that I had some advice: You should stop at "You look great"...It's horrible to get older and have to listen to others' ailments when yours are so much more interesting!

Number 5: This is a wonderful time for each of us to remind ourselves what's really important in life, and what's not.

One of many notes I received after September 11 came from a good friend who was away from home that day. When he got home, he was struck by how trivial the headlines had been in the previous day's paper, still waiting for him on his kitchen counter. "I looked over all the things that were so important Monday and reflected how this act of terror changed our world in just a few seconds." Now all he wanted to do was hug his wife and children and grand-children...

Advice Number 6: It's also a wonderful time to remind ourselves that tolerance is one of the most important of human qualities. We need to learn to appreciate and celebrate the differences in people, rather than fear or resent them. I agree with the teacher who said we could all learn from crayons: Some are sharp, some are pretty, some are dull, some have weird names, and all are different colors, but they all have to learn to live in the same box.

Advice Number 7: Learn not to waste time. That doesn't mean you have to work hard and play hard every single minute. Enjoying a good book, taking a nap on the back porch, watching it rain—we've been getting a lot of practice at this in Houston lately. Anyway, this is all time very well spent.

Staying angry at a friend, worrying about things you can't change, watching reruns on television—those are precious moments lost.

The tragedy of 9/11 presented new challenges for Mrs. Bush when she made public appearances, especially since she preferred making her points with humor. She did what she could to help steady the nerves of a very anxious country. Just ten days later, she spoke at a university in East Stroudsburg, Pennsylvania. Many people from the community commuted every day to New York City; some of them worked in the Twin Towers; some lives were lost.

She had gentle advice for her fragile audience that day, as she did for the country. She even made them smile a time or two:

I'd like to start by congratulating the university— and thanking them—for not canceling this convocation. Certainly all of us in the last week have struggled with how we can help, how we can show our support for the victims of our horrible national tragedy, and how we can make a difference.

I know that is especially true here in this community, like so many others in the region surrounding New York City. I was so sad to learn that some of your friends and neighbors and family lost their lives last week. My deepest sympathy to the victims' families and friends, and to all of you who have experienced this tragedy firsthand. Our thoughts and prayers are with you.

How do you begin picking up the pieces? It will take time, of course, and a lot of courage. But by

coming here tonight, you took an important step. The best thing we can all do right now is get back to some sense of normalcy, to get back to the business of living our lives. It's what's best for each of us personally, and it's what's best for the country. If we stay home and lock our doors, then we will lose even more than what we have already lost.

… In the last week we learned just how big-hearted Americans are. So many people volunteered in so many ways—whether it was to be on the front lines of the rescue effort, to give blood, to donate food and clothing—that finally officials had to politely say, "Okay, we have enough." It certainly was America at her best. The outpouring of love and affection overwhelmed us all and made us proud.

It's so important we carry on that spirit every single day of our lives. I know that community service is an important part of campus life here at East Stroudsburg and that students donated more than eighteen thousand hours of volunteer service. All I can say is keep up the good work. After all, one of the best ways we can help this great country find its footing again is by giving of ourselves to our communities and to each other. Never in our history has it been more important for all of us to become good neighbors.

CHAPTER 5

Read

I truly feel that if more people could read,
write, and comprehend, so many of our
social problems could be solved.

—Barbara Bush

*It was her clarion call for forty years. Barbara Bush never
gave up on her dream that America would become a more
literate country.*

*She talked about literacy to anyone who would listen.
But she did much more than talk. She established a foundation. She visited literacy programs all over the country—
in schools, libraries, community centers, prisons, wherever
people were learning to read. She read to thousands of
children, mostly in person but also by satellite and, in later*

years, through Skype. She mentioned the importance of literacy in every speech she gave, no matter the audience or topic. She helped raise tens of millions of dollars, especially through the annual Celebration of Reading events she and President Bush founded and hosted in Houston, Dallas, Washington, DC, Maryland, Florida, and Maine.

She even had two of her dogs write books, giving all their proceeds to literacy.

She adopted literacy as her cause in 1978, when her husband was thinking about running for president. As she often explained to her audiences, she knew she needed to pick a specific cause, but what? While running in Houston's Memorial Park in the summer of 1978, she thought about all the things that worried her—drugs, teenage pregnancy, homelessness, a growing school dropout rate—and she suddenly realized everything she worried about would be better if more people could read, write, and comprehend. That would mean they would be more likely to stay in school, get a job, have a better life. She had found her cause.

One small problem: She told the campaign staff she had her cause but failed to tell them she knew nothing about literacy. At least not yet.

So it was with great surprise, when she arrived at Cardinal Stritch University in Milwaukee for an event, that she was met by a Sister Camille, who announced they were all gathered to hear her thoughts about literacy.

After a few panicked moments, she looked around the room at all the expectant faces and asked them this question: **If you were married to the president and had the opportunity to really make a dent in the field of illiteracy, what one thing would you do?...Each person, tell me how you would go about it.**

They had so many ideas to offer her, they ran out of time. So out of that experience came, of course, some advice from the future First Lady, which she included at the end of this story:

When in doubt, keep quiet, listen, and let others talk. They'll be happy, and you might learn something.

Mrs. Bush was often frustrated, during the eight years she was the wife of the vice president, by the lack of press attention paid to her cause. C. Fred's Story: A Dog's Life, *a children's book published in 1984 and "written" by the Bushes' dog, helped. But it really annoyed her when hordes of press would come every December when she and usually a grandchild or two put the top on the National Christmas Tree—a job that had been delegated to her by First Lady Nancy Reagan. Where was the press when she was talking literacy?*

Her husband becoming president in 1989 solved the problem of no press interest. She announced her foundation

in March of that year, and she was off and running again. Their new dog Millie "wrote" Millie's Book in 1990, raising more than a million dollars for the foundation.

And she barnstormed the country talking about literacy. Here is some of what she said at a fund-raising dinner for the Lubbock, Texas, Area Literacy Coalition on May 22, 1992:

I'm especially happy to be here to cheer on our growing and thriving literacy coalition. Every single adult learner in this room, and this nation, deserves our deepest admiration and respect.

Nothing takes more courage or persistence or heart than taking a second chance on education. And nothing can have a greater impact on people's lives— at home, on the job, and in the community.

Congratulations, all of you, for showing us it's never too late, or too hard, to learn…I even know a sixty-six-year-old man named George who announced recently that he's going back to school to become computer literate.

…I've talked to all kinds of real people— newcomers struggling with a strange new language; single mothers getting off welfare; factory workers getting on assembly lines; high school dropouts who want to drop back in; and prison inmates who want to get out and stay out.

And I've talked to the CEOs of big and little companies, and civic and education leaders, and mayors and governors, and to students and teachers.

They've all taught me a great deal...And I'd like to emphasize the most important thing I've learned: Literacy is everybody's business. Period.

...Literacy is not just learning to read and write better. It's people making better choices, raising children, doing old and new jobs better, and being better citizens all around.

Mrs. Bush took her bully pulpit with her from the White House to private life. Wherever and to whomever she was asked to speak, she talked about literacy, and her message was always the same: Read. Read to your children. Get involved.

Here is one such speech excerpt:

Each of you in this room has a very important role to play in making our country more literate, since the best place to start is in our own homes. Please remember to read to your children or grandchildren. It helps them develop an imagination, improves their vocabulary, and instills in them an early love of reading.

And don't forget to turn off the TV once in a while. In the United States, the average kindergarten student has seen more than five thousand hours of television. That's more time than it takes to earn a college degree! I agree with Groucho Marx, who once said, "I find television very educational. Whenever someone turns the television on in my house, I go into another room and read a book."

Reading to your children is important for another reason: No matter who you are and what you do, your family must be your number one priority. And there is no better way to spend quality time with your children, and show them love and affection, than to sit with your arms around them as you read to them or they read to you.

So did Barbara Bush make a difference in the world of literacy?

She would say "not enough." She was disappointed more progress had not been made in her lifetime.

To get a more unbiased view, we asked Sharon Darling—president and founder of the National Center for Family Learning (formerly the National Center for Family Literacy); a founding board member of the Barbara Bush Foundation for Family Literacy; and one of Mrs. Bush's early literacy mentors—to look back on her contributions:

Illiteracy was a hidden problem for millions of Americans. It would have stayed hidden—even though we have known for many years that literacy is the fiber of thriving families and communities and the key to future generations—were it not for Barbara Bush. She brought to the forefront the importance of literacy in the workforce, for families to have a sustaining wage, and the importance for human potential and self-worth. She spent the last forty years of her life elevating the visibility of the hidden problems and the urgency for solutions.

She used the bully pulpit but went far beyond. She studied the issue and listened to those on the ground dealing with the problem—practitioners, volunteers, and, most importantly, the adults who were struggling every day. She was certainly interested in the research, but also learning from the research about how to be more effective in reaching and teaching adults who had fallen through the cracks.

While she was the vice president's wife, Barbara influenced President Reagan, who announced an emphasis on adult literacy along with a huge push to enlist volunteers to help. Both ABC and PBS created Literacy USA because of her work, and education secretary William Bennett created an Office of Adult Literacy at the Department of Education, which did great things.

President and Mrs. Bush hosted Literacy Honors

events in the White House to honor champions of literacy and adult literacy students. The event attracted literacy advocates, policy makers, and key officials from the administration and federal agencies. Mrs. Bush always professed to stay away from policy, but her ability to shine a light on the hidden problem of adult literacy and showcase families in need alongside those who had the influence to provide resources was most powerful. Perhaps it is no surprise then that her husband signed the National Literacy Act into law in 1991.

The accomplishments made to create a literate nation during that time were immense, and generations to come will benefit from Barbara Bush's leadership for decades in the future.

She knew that by educating a mother, all her children would be more successful, and those children would have children and they would have more opportunities, and on and on through the generations. The ripple effect of family literacy could indeed change communities and ultimately a nation.

Mrs. Bush always stayed grounded on what was happening out in the field. She loved meeting with the mothers and hearing their stories of hope and courage and their determination to use the opportunity to make a better life for their children. She used humor to put everyone at ease, and the way the mothers opened up to her to share very personal parts of their lives was astounding.

She also had a way of helping the mothers feel valued and admired. She motivated them and congratulated them for taking the steps to learn to read and improve their academic and parenting skills. Many years later when I had a chance to meet some of the previous students of family literacy, many would tell me that it changed their lives. Often, they said that when someone they admired so much believed in them, they began to believe in themselves.

Mrs. Bush believed literacy was a civil right. She helped an entire nation see past the stereotypes of families living in poverty and lacking the skills to climb out. She was able to do that because she respected all people and was authentic in her belief in equity in opportunity for all Americans.

As of today, the Barbara Bush Foundation for Family Literacy has raised and provided more than $110 million in support to create or expand family literacy programs in all fifty states and the District of Columbia.

They are not done yet. As the foundation's president and CEO, British Robinson, says:

As we work to fulfill Barbara Bush's legacy, our calling is to improve lives through literacy. No longer can we allow low literacy to hold back one in every six Americans from fully engaging in our society as parents, workers, and citizens. We are dedicated to expanding access to literacy services for adults nationwide because we believe in the uniquely transformative power of literacy. The ability to read, write, and comprehend brings dignity to daily life and equal opportunity to fulfill one's great potential.

Even into her nineties, Mrs. Bush embraced and pushed for new, innovative ideas to help us become more literate. She was very excited when her foundation partnered with the Dollar General Literacy Foundation and the XPRIZE Foundation to launch a global competition offering millions in cash prizes to anyone from anywhere, regardless of their background, who could develop groundbreaking adult literacy tools for smartphones. Why? Because she knew that there were not nearly enough traditional classroom programs to serve the millions in need, and even if there were, adult learners face unique challenges that often prevent them from getting the help they deserve. She wanted tools that could be available wherever and whenever the adult learners were available.

Although she died before the three-city, twelve-thousand-adult-learner field test concluded, her instincts and perseverance have already paid off. Early results from the smartphone applications developed as part of the endeavor have been very promising. This could revolutionize opportunities for adult learners, and her vision of solving the adult literacy crisis will have taken a major leap forward.

When Barbara Bush died, author James McBride implored all Americans to take her advice on fighting illiteracy in our country. He ended his op-ed piece published by the New York Times *on April 20 with this plea:*

In the last years of her life, she dragged her octogenarian body onto planes and buses and into cars from one end of the country to the other, raising money for her literacy foundation. She despised ignorance. She despised it because she knew it was wrong.

And if you loved her and what she represented, you'll go out and get a book. And you will read it. You will turn off that TV and pay attention. And cut the tweeting. And cut the Facebook chatter and all the other nonsense. And you will get busy doing what Barbara Bush spent most of her life doing. You will fight ignorance. You will learn to love. And in doing so, you will do what she did.

You will change the world.

CHAPTER 6

Homeward Bound

When the end came, she showed us all how
to die with dignity and faith, for she surely
knew that the best was yet to come.
                    —Reverend Russell Levenson

*Shortly before Mrs. Bush died, she decided to come home
from the hospital, stop all medical treatment, and let
nature take its course.*

The world momentarily gasped, then sighed.

But as Dr. Marc Siegel—author, columnist, and professor of medicine—wrote in the Wall Street Journal *the day
before she died:*

Barbara Bush's decision to stop aggressive treatment for lung and heart disease at 92 is a valiant one...now she is facing death with fortitude, courage, and realism. She should inspire everyone in the medical arena, doctors and patients alike.

...She looked soberly at her life and made her decision. A willingness to face more bright lights and blipping monitors in the emergency room and the intensive care unit can seem like courage. But it often comes from fear of dying or the urging of a family member or doctor who doesn't want to let go. It has taken me many years to accept that Mrs. Bush and those like her are the most courageous.

As her health declined, her interest in life did not. Former White House staffer Sondra Haley visited her in the hospital toward the end:

The last opportunity I had to see Mrs. Bush was on Good Friday, about two weeks prior to her passing. She was in the hospital and so was President Bush. Jean [Becker] and I stopped by to see them before heading to church. They were side by side, holding hands in her room. She was on oxygen and needed care but instead of focusing on herself she focused on others.

Her first question: **How is your mom?** I said she was recovering from a broken femur. She quickly responded,

How can you be here? I explained my brother Tim was with her, to which she said: **Then who's taking care of [our family restaurant] Captain Jack's?**

Once she was satisfied that my mom, brother, and restaurant were all okay, she began to say to me over and over **we love you** and **you're beautiful**. It was so very sweet and so unexpected. She was known to be tough and she was. But she was also very generous and thoughtful.

Looking back, I feel she knew she was leaving this earth soon and knew it was our last time together. And quintessential Barbara Bush, she asked about my family and gave me the most beautiful goodbye. One making me feel important to her. One filled with love and affection.

*In the book she wrote with her sister, Jenna—*Sisters First*—granddaughter Barbara Bush talks about the last phone call they made to their Ganny:*

Two days before her death, international media outlets broadcasted that she was expected to die any day. Yet, when Jenna and I three-way-called my grandparents' home, we burst out laughing (and crying) when she was the one to answer the landline. In her usual brash and caring style, she instructed us not to believe everything we read. **They're making it sound like I'm wilting in here!**

Then her voice caught as she went into protector mode: **Don't worry, girls, I won't leave you,** realizing as she completed her sentence that those words weren't true. We cried and cried, our voices quivering as we told her how much we loved her and how we'd head to Houston to see her. Sadly, we didn't make it in time.

Evan Sisley was President Bush's personal aide at the time of Mrs. Bush's death. But as a licensed paramedic and a former navy corpsman with battlefield experience in Afghanistan, Evan oversaw both President and Mrs. Bush's medical care at home and worked closely with their team of doctors.

One funny note: Evan confided in President Bush shortly before his death that Evan's next step in life was medical school. President Bush nodded, said he approved, and told Evan that would be "a good résumé builder." We still smile at that exchange. I am fairly certain he assumed Evan would be president one day. Evan is now pursuing a career in medicine at Georgetown, where his husband, Ian, is studying law.

Evan shared these reflections of watching George and Barbara Bush's final days:

I began working for President and Mrs. Bush five years before they died. Though there are many memories and moments with Mrs. Bush that I will always

cherish, the most important thing I learned from her was by witnessing their relationship at the end of their life.

Their relationship was quiet during those final years. Most everything that they needed to say had been said in over seventy years of marriage. Most of their time was spent watching movies, holding hands, or needle-pointing. Many days were spent devoted to visiting the other in the hospital when they had a medical setback. Though they knew it, at the end of the night they always let the other know that they loved them "more than tongue can tell."

Their devotion to each other was shown in their need to be in each other's orbit. They would separate throughout the day for short stints: his visit to the office, her needlepoint group at church, but they would always rotate back to each other for a meal or to spend several hours together at night, not always talking but just being present with each other.

They were still playful and liked to poke fun at each other even in their nineties. Once when President Bush was doing a breathing treatment, he was waving the nebulizer device while periodically puffing on it from the corner of his mouth like it was a pipe. Mrs. Bush walked in and said, **George, you really must shut your mouth**, encouraging him to properly seal his lips around the device and ingest the medication that was supposed to help him breathe. In standard Bush form, President Bush responded with, "What's good for the goose is good for the gander."

When one of them had a medical setback, the other would spend most of the day visiting them in the hospital. Houston Methodist Hospital started reserving two rooms, knowing that the other would inevitably catch a virus or wear themselves down with the constant trips.

The day before Mrs. Bush died, President Bush wanted to let her know that he understood that she was dying and that it was going to be okay. He went into the living room and said, "Bar, I'm not worried about you." She looked up at him from her chair where she sat needlepointing and said, **I'm not worried about you either, Georgie**. Not a grand statement, but perfect. They spent a life protecting and devoted to each other. They were secure in their faith, and they knew where the other was heading. They just wanted each other to know that it was going to be okay.

On her final day on this earth, Mrs. Bush lay in bed, unable to talk. President Bush sat next to her and held her hand. Quiet, but in each other's orbit. She passed away that evening surrounded by grandchildren, children, and the love of her life, George Bush. He cried quietly, composed himself, and refocused his attention on the other people in the room. He didn't want his family to see him cry; he didn't want them to worry about him either.

They believed in life devoted to the service of others and their devotion to each other was the finest example of that creed. Barbara Bush showed me, not by words but by example, how to be a spouse, how to be the fierce protector of another human being while also putting their needs before your own. Actions speak louder than words, and President and Mrs. Bush showed their devotion to each other "more than tongue can tell."

CHAPTER 7

Reflections

We began Pearls of Wisdom *with five essays written by Barbara Bush's five children.*

We will end with some essays written by a few of her close friends, some of whom had a hard time with their assignment for the book: "Send us a paragraph or two about what you learned from her." We decided they deserved dispensation, and you deserve to read what they wrote. In alphabetical order:

"SHE MADE MY MAMA PROUD"
BY AUTHOR JILL CONNER BROWNE
(AKA THE SWEET POTATO QUEEN)

It is said that our "good" lives on after us and for no one is that more true than for Barbara Bush.

Through her generous and tireless efforts to bring literacy to the world, my own home state of Mississippi (top of all the bad lists, bottom of all the good) has been blessed in many ways.

Teen Trendsetters, a program sponsored by her literacy foundation, in particular has had profound effects, not only in the target area of literacy but perhaps even more importantly in RELATIONSHIPS between races and socioeconomic classes. Barriers are being obliterated. We are even seeing a whole group of our teen mentors being inspired to pursue careers in teaching as a direct result of the successes they have helped achieve with their mentees.

But as laudable as all that is, it is not what will endear Barbara Bush to me for the rest of my life.

My love and gratitude toward her are deeply personal. My books are often referred to as "spicy" and my mama was genuinely appalled by them. The success of them did nothing to appease her. But in 2006, when I was first invited to speak for the Celebration of Reading in Florida, and I returned home with a photograph of myself and my husband with President and Mrs. Bush—well, honey, suffice it to say the TIDE TURNED. Mama wore that photo OUT, showing it to any and all who came within three feet of her.

With a lump in my throat and tears in my eyes to this very day, I tell you that I will love Barbara Bush forevermore for making my mama proud of me.

"FIRST AMONG FIRST LADIES" BY AUTHOR MARY HIGGINS CLARK

It is hard to write about Barbara Bush and think about her in the past tense. She was keenly intelligent, warm, friendly, hardworking, direct, and overall a magnificent human being.

My friendship with Barbara resulted from a reporter asking her a question. "Whose books do you like to read?" She immediately answered, "Maeve Binchy and Mary Higgins Clark." Delighted, I wrote her a thank-you note. I promptly received an invitation to a state dinner at the White House.

When I arrived, a handsome young Marine was designated as my escort. Cocktails were being served in the East Room. A few minutes later we were gently urged to form a semicircle. The familiar "Hail to the Chief" was played as President Bush and Barbara entered the room. After each guest had been greeted by the First Couple, the doors were opened, and all were invited into the dining room.

Barbara loved to surround herself with interesting

people from many different fields. I was seated at her table and introduced myself to the man in the chair next to me.

"Chuck Heston," he responded, extending his hand.

"As in Charlton Heston?" I asked.

"I'm so glad you recognize my name," he said with a smile.

"Everyone knows your name," I replied as my mind was filled with the image of Moses, holding his staff aloft, parting the Red Sea.

Barbara's keen interest in literature and promoting literacy cemented our budding friendship. She once asked me to fly with her to visit a grade school in Houston that was being named after her. That evening we had dinner in town, and I found the name I wanted for the lead character in my new book. It was the restaurant owner's name, Carlie.

My daughter Carol and I once stayed over at the Bushes' home in Houston. Showing us around, she walked us down to the bedroom she and George shared, and opened the door of the large closet. The sight of neat rows of clothing, some folded, others on hangers, was impressive. She picked up a long stick and deftly unhooked a wildly colored cowboy shirt from the top rack. "Is this the ugliest thing you've ever seen?" she asked. "Can you believe George wears this?" We all laughed. When Barbara had told the president what she thought of the shirt, he'd said plaintively, "Bar, I don't make fun of your clothes."

Another time we were both in Los Angeles, and I realized we were staying in the same hotel, so I phoned her. She immediately invited me to come up and have tea. A few minutes later a maître d' arrived, followed by four waiters with a silver tray.

You may pour, Barbara told the maître d'. She looked down at the cups and then back at him in astonishment. **You're pouring water!** she exclaimed.

"The tea bag follows," he said proudly as his assistant came forward, dangling a tea bag on a string. After they filed out, Barbara murmured, **I'm so glad the queen isn't here.**

At an annual literary gathering in Houston, Barbara invited me, Larry McMurtry, and some other writers to lunch in their home. While seated, the president began feeding scraps from the table to their dog Millie. A disapproving Barbara looked at him and shook her head. **George, if that dog gets sick in the middle of the night, you'll be the one to get up with her!**

The last time I saw Barbara I was among the many guests who attended her ninetieth birthday celebration in Kennebunkport. Surrounded by four generations of her family, she looked radiant and spoke warmly to the assembled guests. She died almost three years later. For me, she'll always be the "First" among "First Ladies."

"SON"
BY WILLIAM JEFFERSON CLINTON 42ND PRESIDENT OF THE UNITED STATES

I liked and admired Barbara from the first time I met her in 1983, when she and then vice president Bush hosted a cookout in Kennebunkport for all the nation's governors and our families. She and George were both kind and welcoming to us, and I could tell from the very beginning that she was smart, witty, and tough.

Over the years we maintained a friendly, respectful relationship—I'll always be grateful for her grace and graciousness toward my family after the 1992 election—but it wasn't until well after my presidency, once George and I worked together to spearhead American relief efforts in the wake of the South Asian tsunami of 2004 and later Hurricane Katrina, that we truly became close. Even then, it took me a little longer to win her over than it did George.

I'll never forget the moment I realized I had finally broken through with her. In May of 2005, we held a big outdoor event in Houston to announce our fund-raising progress for tsunami relief. It was Barbara's job to introduce me and George. When it came time, she said, **It's my great honor to introduce America's favorite new couple. Everyone is talking about the Odd Couple, George and Bill—or as I now call him, Son.** When I got up to speak, I joked that every family, if it's big enough like the Bush clan, has at least one black sheep who wanders off.

After that day, I realized that Barbara and I had become real friends. I treasured my annual summer trips to Kennebunkport to spend time with her and George. Until the end, during all those wonderful visits, I knew she was just looking at her black sheep thinking, "I've got your number, but I like you anyway." And I knew she meant it.

"THE BEST LUCY & ETHEL OF ALL TIME"
BY AUTHOR BRAD MELTZER

Barbara Bush gave me one of the most amazing, rewarding, and unimaginable friendships of my entire life. When we first met, I was utterly intimidated by the raw power that came off her. I left thinking two things: (1) She's the reason the Bush family took the White House twice. And (2) I never want to be on her bad side. But I also instantly knew this: She was so damn funny. I mean it. As sharp a wit as I've ever seen. She wrote in one of her biographies that while she was shopping for one of my books, someone in a bookstore told her she looked like Barbara Bush. I don't remember the punchline anymore. But she had the perfect punchline. Always.

Soon after, we started writing to each other. Our letters kept going back and forth over the years, hers always handwritten. When I started writing biographies of famous people for children, she wrote to me about how she saw Amelia Earhart up close—and then added in the PS that she didn't meet Lincoln, but that she felt just as old. I wrote her back saying that that was funny, but that we all knew she met George Washington. The woman got good comedy. She was my favorite pen pal ever.

Of course, one of my favorite moments with her was when I got to take my mom to meet her. It was when my mom was sick. I knew the end was coming. Of course, Mrs. Bush treated my mom like royalty— and gave me one of the last great beautiful meals I ever had with my mother. After that, she'd always ask me about how my mom was. And she'd always remember the story I told the very first time I met her: about how many books my mom sold for me. Indeed, during one of my last visits with Mrs. Bush, right before the past election, she recounted the story perfectly to me. You see, Mrs. Bush knew the power of a strong mother.

And she also knew the power of literacy. She dedicated her life to books—and to making sure people could read them: the poor, immigrants new to our country, people who just couldn't learn. The Barbara Bush Foundation for Family Literacy has raised and is still raising millions of dollars to help others unlock the most powerful weapons in the universe: books and ideas. When my kids were born, she told me to read to them. She told me it wasn't the story that mattered— it was being that close and sharing that time together. As always, she was right.

Her love for literacy lasted so long, she turned her ninetieth birthday party into a fund-raiser for literacy. When she told me she was asking four authors to entertain there, I was like, "Wow! Who're you getting?" She was like, **Dummy, it's you.** It was my true honor to entertain at that event and stand next to her as she blew out the candles.

And of course, there was our craziest and best moment of all: She and I re-creating *I Love Lucy*'s chocolate conveyor belt scene. We really did it— me eating hundreds of chocolates in President Bush's office. Why'd she do it? Because it was for literacy, for kids—and of course, because it was damn funny. She did it all in one take. Forever a pro.

My God, the world is already quieter today without her in it. Mrs. Bush, thank you for what you've done for all those young readers out there. Thank you for empowering all those who needed to find their own power. And thank you for a friendship I will never forget.

"A TRUE AND VALUED FRIEND" BY MILA MULRONEY FIRST LADY OF CANADA, 1984–1993

I met Barbara Bush when Brian and I paid a visit to Washington, shortly after Brian became Leader of the Opposition in Canada.

Barbara hosted a luncheon for me in the vice president's residence. It could not have been a livelier or more welcoming affair. She thought of everything and took into consideration my age and inexperience.

When I first arrived, Barbara met me at the door. She personally made sure that I was introduced to everyone and that those introductions would facilitate our conversations. Barbara's personality and pride in her position and role were very clear to me that day.

The Naval Observatory was in all its glory. The

sun was shining through the many windows. The table was set with beautiful flowers and in front of each guest there was a porcelain replica of the vice president's home filled with dried flowers from the garden. Of the twelve invitees, Barbara included Tipper Gore and Strom Thurmond's wife, Nancy Moore, as well as Laura Bush to ensure most everyone was close to me in age.

Barbara was easy to get to know. She was frank and friendly. She was interested and interesting. Most of all, she was engaging and insightful to talk to. For me, it was a pleasure to be in her company.

As time passed and I got to know Barbara, she became a true and valued friend, someone I trusted implicitly. One of her greatest qualities was her frankness. From her, I always knew that I would receive the unvarnished truth. She could be tough and courageous and determined, all the while enjoying every moment to the fullest.

For the rest of Barbara's incredible life, we were close friends. She and her husband, George, were at the opening of the Canadian Embassy in Washington with us. We were together almost every September in Kennebunkport, walking the dogs on the beach, singing with Jimmy Dean while his wife played the piano. Barbara flew to Ottawa in a blizzard to attend a fund-raiser I was holding at the Museum of Civilization, for cystic fibrosis. We went to Greece to spend a week with them cruising through the Greek islands several times. The time we had together flew by much too quickly. They were truly unforgettable.

I am very sad that she is gone. I know that I was extremely fortunate to have had a friend and a mentor like Barbara Bush. I learned a great deal from such an incredible person. I shall never forget her kindness and friendship.

"YOU WRETCHED RASCAL"
BY ALAN SIMPSON
FORMER SENATOR FROM WYOMING

When I was teaching at Harvard in the late 1990s and early 2000 (I know how absurd that sounds because I couldn't have gotten into Harvard if I'd picked the locks!) I had received a very secret and confidential message that Barbara Bush's seventy-fifth birthday was on the horizon and the communication indicated that she knew nothing of the "surprise." At that time of my life, I was teaching, lecturing, speaking around the country, and generally irritating people, which was my usual wont! In looking at my calendar, I realized that there was this "item" regarding a birthday for Barbara.

I had a conflict, and knew I couldn't make it, so I called her (you can see where this leads!).

I said, "Barbara, I'm sorry I can't make that party but I hope it's a good one." And she said, **Wait a minute, Al, what are you talking about? What party?**

I said, "Oh, well"—mumble, mumble—"I don't know, somebody told me there was some kind of a function or something" (realizing then that the quicksand was quickly drawing me deeper into the muck). Finally she said, using THAT voice: **I have no idea what you're up to, but if you're up to some trick, you'll pay for this.**

I said, "No, no. Uh, just checking." And she stated, **I'll be watching you!**

Days later I saw her and there could never be a more graphic description of a diminutive silver-haired lady almost grabbing me by my throat and the lapels of my sport coat and admonishing, **You really blew that one, didn't you, Al? The whole family kept the secret, but not you, and I won't forget that!** And she never did! I'll tell you that for sure!

Even for a few years after that she'd grimace and say, **You wretched rascal. You ruined the whole thing.** I finally sheepishly said, "Look, Barbara, the guilt for me is overpowering." She responded briskly with that twinkle in her eye: **Al, guilt is the gift that keeps on giving!**

Yet she was always there for me, especially when I'd get clobbered around on the Bork hearing, or the Thomas hearings.[10] She was always ready with a big hug and a kiss—and I loved that woman. And the reason was, I knew she surely loved me as I loved her, even though, as I say, she could easily forgive, but never forget. I'm living proof of that! God love her!

This is my long way of saying what I learned from her more than anything else is: **the power of forgiving even if you can't forget**.

"GETTING TO KNOW A PRESIDENT AND FIRST LADY" BY DEBBIE SMITH WIFE OF GOSPEL ROCK SINGER MICHAEL W. SMITH

Michael and I met President and Barbara Bush at the taping of a *Christmas in Washington* program. We were a mixture of nerves and excitement when Michael

---

10   Senator Simpson is referring to two controversial Supreme Court nominations: Robert Bork, nominated by Ronald Reagan in 1987; and Clarence Thomas, nominated by George H. W. Bush in 1991. Judge Bork was not confirmed; Justice Thomas was. Senator Simpson, as a member of the Senate Judiciary Committee, played a leading role in both hearings.

accepted—of course—the invitation to sing on the annual televised Christmas show in 1989. In a suit, with his hair flowing over his shoulders, Michael sang his version of "Angels We Have Heard on High" with a local high school choir backing him up. I kept glancing at the Bushes. What were they thinking about this Christian rocker jazzing up a traditional Christmas hymn? And what about that hair?

As the artists who had performed that evening gathered onstage for a final bow, the Bushes came onto the stage to greet each one. Mrs. Bush grabbed Michael's hand and whispered in his ear, **We loved you the most!** Whew. Relief! They didn't hate it! In fact, before we knew it, we were on our way to the White House later that evening, along with all the other artists who had performed. I was literally pinching myself as we sped along in the motorcade, running all the lights and pulling up to the White House. How could this be happening?!

We were treated to a brief tour of the main floor by the president and First Lady themselves. Walking into the East Room, President Bush turned to Michael and said, "Would you like to lead us in some Christmas carols?" as he motioned to the massive grand piano against the wall. Michael winces now at what he asked the president, obviously trying to say something witty: "Is it in tune, Mr. President?"

"I hope so!" was the reply.

After singing around the nicely tuned piano with everyone making beautiful music except for a few of us, we headed up to the private quarters at the First Couple's invitation. Now I was REALLY pinching myself! Michael and I took the elevator with the president and something happened that I will not easily forget but saw repeated over and over in the twenty-nine years of friendship that followed. As soon as we entered the elevator, President Bush greeted the elevator operator by name. "How's your wife doing after her operation?" he questioned, and as we rode up, they continued to chat. The president and Mrs. Bush thanked him for the ride as we got off and I'll have to admit, Michael and I were surprised at their concern and how well they seemed to know this gentleman. Surely that was unusual. Was he a relative or something?

Before long in our friendship we learned that the way they treated the elevator operator was nothing unusual. They treated everyone with respect and concern. It was one of many reasons that endeared them to their staff and security, to family and friends, and to the nation. They were genuine! Added to that, they didn't take themselves too seriously and seemed more interested in the person in front of them than in themselves. Their sense of fun put people at ease. Overall, they loved well and were well loved. At the White House family Christmas brunch four years later—after President Bush had lost the election and just a few weeks before the Bushes would leave the White House—Michael and I noticed that the staff and kitchen employees were very emotional. There were few dry eyes. We overheard some of them saying how much they would miss the Bushes and how they were treated like family. By that time, we could say we knew that feeling as well!

"SOMETHING YOU MIGHT NOT KNOW ABOUT BARBARA BUSH" BY DR. LOUIS SULLIVAN FORMER PRESIDENT OF THE MOREHOUSE SCHOOL OF MEDICINE FORMER SECRETARY OF HEALTH AND HUMAN SERVICES

In November 1982 I met Barbara Bush. She and I were members of a US delegation on a two-week trip to eight countries in sub-Saharan Africa, led by Vice President George H. W. Bush. I was president and dean of Morehouse School of Medicine in Atlanta, a young, predominantly African American medical school whose mission included increasing the racial and ethnic diversity of the health professions in America.

During this two-week trip I learned about Barbara's mission to increase adult literacy so individuals could lead fuller, more enriched, more productive lives, and could achieve financial independence. Barbara spent time meeting with adult groups in Nigeria, Kenya, Zambia, Zimbabwe, and Zaire (now the Democratic Republic of Congo), stressing the importance of improving adult literacy in these countries—many of which had only recently achieved independence from European countries, including Britain and Belgium. Access to an educational program for the general population in these countries had not been a priority of the colonial governments.

I was pleased and excited when Barbara accepted my invitation for her to join the board of trustees of Morehouse School of Medicine. I indicated to her that, since Morehouse School of Medicine had been founded only seven years earlier (in 1975) by Morehouse College, the school had very few alumni, a short history, and faced a major challenge to raise the funds needed for the development of the medical school.

Barbara was a very active, loyal, and productive trustee for Morehouse School of Medicine during her tenure, from January 1983 until January 1989. She missed only one meeting during that six-year period. For the medical school's first national fund campaign in 1984–85, Barbara was the featured speaker at our luncheons in cities across the country, including Boston, Chicago, St. Louis, Minneapolis, Houston, San Francisco, and Miami. With a campaign goal of fifteen million dollars, we raised more than eighteen million.

On campus, Barbara enjoyed interacting with our medical students and our faculty. She was always curious about their background, their goals, and their studies, including their research projects and plans for their careers.

In 1997, Morehouse School of Medicine developed a neuroscience research center, the first such center based at a historically black college or university (HBCU). Morehouse School of Medicine was fortunate to receive a grant from a private foundation to endow the professorship for the neuroscience center: The Barbara and George H. W. Bush Chair of Neuroscience was held by Dr. Peter MacLeish, the founder of the institute. I was particularly pleased and proud when Barbara and President Bush both received honorary degrees from Morehouse School of Medicine for their support of the institution.

Barbara also wrote the foreword to the institution's history: *The Morehouse Mystique: Becoming a Doctor at the Nation's Newest African American Medical School*, published in 2012 by the Johns Hopkins University Press. In the foreword she stated: "I am so proud of the school's remarkable accomplishments and am grateful to have been a part of it during the beginning."

Everyone at Morehouse School of Medicine was excited when Barbara came, for trustees' meetings or on other occasions. I was particularly amused by the number of our female faculty, staff, and students who appeared on campus on those days, wearing triple-stranded pearl necklaces.

It was very clear that she was welcome—indeed beloved—at Morehouse School of Medicine. She left a distinguished legacy with her support for Morehouse School of Medicine and did more than she likely realized to promote diversity and race equality in our medical professions.

"REMEMBER WE LOVE YOU" BY JOHN SUNUNU FORMER GOVERNOR OF NEW HAMPSHIRE FORMER WHITE HOUSE CHIEF OF STAFF

I was the lucky recipient of many pearls of wisdom from Barbara Bush. Sometimes she delivered them as a simply stated good rule for living, and sometimes she shared them by how deftly she handled delicate situations.

One of her message moments for me happened during the week running up to the critical 1988 New Hampshire primary election. I was governor and chair of the vice president's campaign in the state. The vice president had lost badly in Iowa to both Bob Dole and Pat Robertson, and although the Bushes and the campaign were understandably down, in New Hampshire we were ready and confident that we could turn it all around.

Over the first couple of days back in our state it looked like George Bush had regained some momentum, but Bob Dole had responded with some hard-hitting TV ads. Going into the weekend before the Tuesday vote, the Bush campaign gathered to review where we stood. Dole had ramped up the tough tone of his campaign rhetoric, and his ads seemed to be moving voters.

On Friday we met to make the decision on whether to run an anti-Dole TV ad that Roger Ailes had put together, stressing the softness of Dole's position on taxes. George Bush was reluctant to run a strong negative ad. Lee Atwater and I and Roger were all in favor. The vice president couldn't make up his mind. Barbara Bush listened a few minutes to the back-and-forth and clearly sensed her husband's desire not to be seen as demeaning his campaign by going negative on TV. She processed it all quickly, and then said to her husband: **It's okay, George. Let's go with it.** With that she lifted the burden of uncertainty and indecision from the vice president's shoulders.

Barbara Bush's message was clear. The lesson was clear: There is power in the unconditional support of those whom you love and trust. That pearl of wisdom underscored the importance and value of going all in—of communicating in a clear and timely way to free what has to be done without the burden of having to carry the anchor of doubt in the process. In that short, clear message of approval, Barbara Bush reenergized and rededicated George Bush to move forward with a focused message that won the election four days later.

Barbara Bush also delivered a pearl of wisdom to me on my last day in the White House. The president and First Lady and I had become close over the past decade. Of course, I continued to feel close and loyal to them both, but since I was stepping down as chief of staff after three plus years in the White House, it would've been presumptuous to just assume that there would be no change in our relationship.

As my last day was coming to a close, the president and Barbara came down to see me off. We all reminisced a bit and said our goodbyes. Then Barbara put her hands on my shoulders, looked me directly in the eye, and said, **Remember, we love you.** Simple, clear, and unreserved. That pearl of wisdom demonstrated the importance of leaving no doubt about feelings and caring. A simple statement of commitment can reaffirm a relationship for a lifetime.

"THE PEARL AND THE OYSTER" BY DAME ARABELLA WARBURTON CHIEF OF STAFF TO SIR JOHN MAJOR

Within moments of my very first visit to Walker's Point, it was clear just what an extraordinary couple the Bushes were.

I had only ever met them once before—during their official visit to the United Kingdom when he was still president. Here I was years later, as a staffer to the former prime minister, entering the private sanctuary of a man who had once been the most powerful one on the planet, and his wife, the "fearsome" Barbara Bush. This was not a normal sleepover.

As the cars pulled up at the main house, President and Mrs. Bush walked out of the front door to greet Sir John and Dame Norma. Mrs. Bush then turned almost immediately toward me, took my hand in hers, welcomed me with those twinkling eyes, and said **George, you show John and Norma to their cottage, I'll take care of Arabella.** And she did. Even with a household of staff on hand, it was that "fearsome" First Lady who escorted this rather nervous underling to her guest cottage, which was exquisitely stylish, yet modest and cozy with no flash or swank. **We can hear the ocean from this side, the best lullaby in the world.**

I was lucky enough to return to Walker's Point on many occasions during the post-office years of this American president and British prime minister, but luckier still to really get to know the Bushes. My nerves soon dissipated, which encouraged Mrs. Bush to become ever more feisty. She would throw her arms up in horror when she saw my luggage come out of the car. **The only person I know who brings more bags than you is Mila Mulroney. I can't think what the two of you find to pack.**

Mrs. Bush never took any hostages—you knew exactly where you stood with her. Sometimes, I think she felt obliged to live up to her reputation. But even at her most provocative, those twinkling eyes would remove the sting from any censure. The only creatures exempt from her ire were her beloved dogs. On one visit I lost a pile of written postcards. We looked high and low—yet they were nowhere to be found. I then noticed something white sticking out from underneath one of the rugs, which, when lifted, exposed a bundle of chewed-up paper. "Oh no!" we both exclaimed, before Mrs. Bush added: **Millie just loves that game.** The ultimate role model for girl power: strong, determined, and rock solid in every way, but with a marshmallow heart.

We have all been asked for "pearls of wisdom" from Barbara Bush, but her wisdom is indivisible from the oyster shell that was wrapped around her for seventy-three years: George H. W. Bush. What made them so wise? What made them so special? Because he once held the most powerful office in the world? Because of their awe-inspiring political and diplomatic antennae? Because of their limitless energy and love of life? Because of their lifelong sense of purpose and public duty? Well, perhaps all of these things. But what made them super special was that, from the moment you met them—whoever you were, wherever you came from, whatever your status in life—you would be swathed in the same warm, welcoming embrace of two truly exceptional human beings, whose grace, charm, and humor were tangible and pervasive. They were, quite simply, a joy to be around.

Houston may have been their home, but I always thought of Kennebunkport as their soul, where they created a refuge out of their own image: exquisitely stylish, yet modest and cozy—and never, absolutely never, with any flash or swank.

One last thought: Having been reflecting on the brilliant title for this book, I remembered something I learned many moons ago. An oyster never survives much beyond its pearls being removed, for it can never again produce anything that is as luminescent or beautiful. The Pearl and the Oyster. Indivisible to the end.

We will give the final word to the four people who really did have the final word—the three eulogists and the homilist at her funeral on April 21, 2018, at St. Martin's Episcopal Church, Houston.

JON MEACHAM

About a decade ago, I was on the Washington Mall for the National Book Festival, on my way to deliver a talk, when a woman ran up to me—which doesn't happen enough, believe me. She said, "Oh my God, it's you!" I said, "Well, yes." She said, "Oh, I'm so thrilled to meet you. I so admire you. Will you stay right here while I go buy your book? Will you sign it for me?" I said, "Yes, ma'am," feeling, I must admit, quite full of myself. All was right with the world. Then my admirer came back—hand to God—with John Grisham's latest novel.

That had been on a September afternoon, and I was due in Maine the next day to see the forty-first president and Mrs. Bush. Feeling rather sorry for myself, I told them the story. Mrs. Bush shook her head sadly and looked me in the eye. I was ready for motherly reassurance when she said: **Well, how do you think poor John Grisham would feel? You know, he's a very handsome man.**

So I was 0 and 2. But it was a fair, funny point—as were so many of the points Barbara Pierce Bush made in her long and consequential life. Known as Barbara, as Bar, as Mom, as Mother, as Ganny, as the Silver Fox, and as the Enforcer, she was candid and comforting, straightforward and steadfast, honest and loving.

Barbara Bush was the First Lady of the Greatest Generation. As the fiancée and then the wife of a World War II naval aviator, she waited and prayed in the watches of the night. During the war she worked at a nuts-and-bolts factory in Port Chester, New York, doing her part. And she joined George H. W. Bush in the great adventure of postwar Texas, moving to distant Odessa seventy summers ago. (From Rye, her mother sent her boxes of soap and detergent on the grounds that they probably didn't have such things in West Texas.) Mrs. Bush raised a family, lost a daughter to leukemia, and kept everything—and everyone—together. And as the wife of one president and as the mother of another, she holds a distinction that belongs to only one other American: Abigail Adams, who was present at the creation.

From the White House to Camp David to Walker's Point, in hours of war and of peace, of tumult and of calm, the Bushes governed with congeniality, with civility, and with grace. Instinctively generous, Barbara and George Bush put country above party, the common good above political gain, and service to others above the settling of scores.

The couple had met at a Christmas dance in Greenwich in 1941, not quite three weeks after Pearl Harbor. She was wearing a red-and-green holiday dress; he endeavored to get introduced. She was sixteen; he was seventeen. He was the only boy she ever kissed. Her children, she remarked, always wanted to throw up when they heard that. In a letter to Barbara during the war, George H. W. Bush wrote: "I love you, precious, with all my heart and to know that you love me means my life. How often I have thought about the immeasurable joy that will be ours someday. How lucky our children will be to have a mother like you."

I once asked President Bush if he had known, in the beginning, how resilient Mrs. Bush would be. "No," he said, tears coming to his eyes. He went on: "She's the rock of the family, the leader of the family. I kind of float above it all, but she's always there, for me and for the kids. Just amazing. Debutante from Rye, willing to make our own way, have adventures. Wasn't always easy for her, but never a word of complaint—just love, and strength. Opinions too, of course. Lots of those."

She *was* strength itself—and if her tongue was sometimes sharp, she was as honest with herself as she was with others. When she once unwisely described a female political opponent of her husband's as a word that rhymed with "rich," she reported her family had started referring to her as the "Poet Laureate." And she loved the story of how, when her eldest son, the forty-third president, took up painting, his instructor asked him if he'd ever used the color "burnt umber." No, Bush 43 replied, but he *did* remember that from his mother's cooking. **Brings down the house,** she'd say, approvingly. Mother and son needled each other to the end. In her final days, while the forty-third president was visiting, Mrs. Bush asked one of the doctors if they'd like to know why George W. was the way he was, announcing: **I smoked and drank while I was pregnant with him.**

She was a point of light. In 1989, when many Americans lived in ignorance about HIV/AIDS, Mrs. Bush went to a home for infected infants and hugged the children there, as well as an adult male with AIDS. The images sent a powerful message—one of compassion, of love, of acceptance.

She believed literacy a fundamental civil and human right and gave the cause her all. At a televised event commemorating the bicentennial of the Constitution, Mrs. Bush met a man named J. T. Pace, the sixty-three-year-old son of a former sharecropper. Mr. Pace, who had only recently become literate, was scheduled to read the Constitution's preamble aloud. Backstage, he was nervous. Mrs. Bush asked if it would help if they read it together on the broadcast. Mr. Pace agreed. Soon the two of them stood onstage, reading in unison. As Mr. Pace grew comfortable, Mrs. Bush lowered her voice—and lowered it again—and then again—until at last he was reading wholly on his own. He wept, and he read—supported by Barbara Bush, who stood to the side, now silent. Her work was done as his voice spoke of the unending search for a more perfect Union. J. T. Pace had found his voice in part because Barbara Bush had lent him her heart.

Just last summer, on a sunny afternoon on the Bushes' porch in Maine, talk turned to World War II and that terrible Saturday, September 2, 1944, when Lieutenant (junior grade) George H. W. Bush was shot down on a bombing raid over Chichijima. Two of his crewmates didn't make it, becoming casualties of war. Lieutenant Bush parachuted out of the bomber, plunged into the sea, came up to the surface, flopped onto his life raft, and waited, scared and retching. Had young Bush been captured by the Japanese, he would have been held captive on an island that was home to horrific war crimes—including cannibalism. ("Bar," he'd say in later years, "I could've been an hors d'oeuvre.") It had been the closest of calls.

George, Mrs. Bush said that day in Maine last July, in their great old age, lost in reminiscence, **you must have been saved for a reason. I know there had to be a reason.**

President Bush sat silently for the briefest of moments, then raised that big left hand and pointed his finger across the table at his wife. "*You*," he said hoarsely. "*You* were the reason."

SUSAN BAKER

It's hard to think of life without the "force of nature" that was our dear friend Barbara Bush. She was smart, strong, fun, and feisty—even sometimes making a headline she later regretted! The world saw that, and like we did, they admired and loved her for it.

The world also saw a remarkable and selfless companion to her beloved husband, George. It was extraordinary how she managed their rambunctious household in thirty different homes in seventeen cities! At the same time, she fully participated in his amazing career—including too many political campaigns to count—starting from the time he was chairman of the Harris County Republican Party to becoming president of the United States. Once back in Houston, they continued their dedication to volunteerism, and exhausting rounds of good works. Rather than bemoan their many moves, Barbara just laughed and said, **One thing I can say about George: He may not be able to keep a job, but he's certainly not boring.**

The world saw a compassionate but strict mother who inspired her children with tender love and firm lessons—and when needed, the fear of God. When we saw her and George together with their five children, and with their seventeen grandchildren and [eight] great-grands, we knew that they represented the very best. As we watched their brood wisecrack with one another, or work together on a volunteer program or campaign, we thought how wonderful it would be if more families could be so cohesive. Barbara, the tough but loving Enforcer, was the secret sauce of this extraordinary family.

The world respects Barbara Bush's deep passion and great effectiveness in equipping those who cannot read with the skill to do so. We all celebrate her vision and tenacious dedication to literacy!

Of course, the world has seen Barbara's many public contributions, but what the world may not have seen is what an amazing, caring, and beautiful friend that Bar was to so many of us.

When Jim and I first arrived in Washington in 1975, I was overwhelmed trying to manage our newly blended family of seven children in an intimidating environment. Fortunately, Bar took me under her wing. She encouraged me, she offered suggestions, and she invited us to lunch almost every Sunday. Those hamburger lunches (that always ended with a fabulous dessert!) included famous personalities as well as many "unknowns" whom they loved, and this really helped us become part of the Washington world.

When we returned to Washington in 1981, George was vice president and Jim was White House chief of staff. Bar encouraged me to use Jim's position in the Reagan administration to promote the causes I cared about. This really pushed me out of my comfort zone, but I followed her wise lead.

She supported my efforts to help the homeless by holding meetings in the vice president's house. What a blessing! This meant that many came who otherwise would NOT have given our group the time of day! She also hosted controversial homeless advocates so we could help people understand the plight of those living on the streets, even though that was not a popular position in the administration. Bar taught us volumes about who our neighbors are, and how to love them.

Because of their own tragic loss of daughter Robin, Barbara knew how to comfort those who were suffering. My Jim was among them, as she helped him during his first wife's losing battle with cancer. Barbara's motivation to help others was never about herself, but about giving love and support to those in need.

Her friendships didn't stop with people she knew. Barbara Bush was pen pals with people she never met. She corresponded for several years with a young girl who named her heifer after Barbara. The child sent her frequent updates on the bovine Barbara Bush, which competed in the Houston Rodeo and Livestock Show one year and finished in eighth place. **I was sorry for my little friend**, Barbara later said, **but was slightly relieved, as I'm not sure I could have stood the headlines: BARBARA BUSH WINS THE FAT STOCK SHOW!**

About friendship, Bar said, **The most important yardstick of your success will be how you treat other people—your family, friends, and co-workers, and even strangers you meet along the way.** She was the gold standard of what it meant to be a friend, because she was motivated by the desire to show God's love to each and every one of His children she met.

C. S. Lewis once defined friendship as "the instrument by which God reveals to each of us the beauties of others." Bar's beauty was in evidence every day of her life.

Saying goodbye to our special friend is painful, but there is great comfort in knowing that we will see this "good and faithful servant" again one day. Thank you, dear Lord, for bringing Barbara Pierce Bush, this vibrantly beautiful human being, into the world, and especially for bringing her friendship into our lives.

GOVERNOR JEB BUSH

As I stand here today, to share a few words about my mom, I feel her looming presence behind me.

I know exactly what she is thinking right now.

Jeb, keep it short. Don't drag this out. People have heard enough remarks already. And, most of all, don't get weepy. Remember, I've spent decades laughing and living a life with these people!

And that is true.

Barbara Bush filled our lives with laughter and joy, and in the case of her family, she was our teacher and role model on how to live a life of purpose and meaning.

On behalf of our family, we want to thank the thousands and thousands of expressions of condolence and love for our precious mother.

We want to thank Mom's caregivers for their compassionate care in the last months of her life.

I want to thank Neil and Maria for their next-door family love of our parents.

We want to thank Jon and Susan for their eloquent words. Meacham, you might have been a little long, but it was beautiful!

We want to thank Russ [Levenson] and Laura for their friendship and pastoral care of our parents.

And we want to thank all who are gathered here to celebrate the life of Barbara Bush.

It is appropriate to express gratitude because we learned to do that at a very early age. You see, our mom was our first and most important teacher.

Sit up.

Look people in the eye.

Say "please" and "thank you."

Do your homework.

Quit whining and stop complaining.

Eat your broccoli. Yes, Dad, she said that.

The little things we learned became habits, and they led to bigger things like:

Be kind.

Always tell the truth.

Serve others.

Treat everyone as you would want to be treated.

And love your God with your heart and soul.

What a blessing to have a teacher like that 24-7!

To be clear, her students weren't perfect. (That's an understatement!)

Mom got us through our difficult times with consistent take-it-to-the-bank unconditional, but tough, love.

She called her style a "benevolent dictatorship," but honestly it wasn't always benevolent.

When our children got a little older, they would spend more time visiting their Gampy and Ganny. All it would take was one week and when they came home, all of a sudden, they were pitching in around the house, they didn't fight as much, and they were actually nice to be with!

I attribute this to the unbridled fear of the "Ganny lecture" and the habit-forming effects of better behavior taking hold.

Even in her nineties, Mom could strike fear into her grandchildren, nephews, nieces, and her children if someone didn't behave.

There were no safe spaces or micro-aggressions allowed with Barbara Pierce Bush. But in the end, every grandchild knew their Ganny loved them.

We learned a lot *more* from our mom and our Ganny.

We learned not to take ourselves too seriously.

We learned that humor is a joy that should be shared. Some of my greatest memories are participating in our family dinners where Mom would get into it, most of the time with George W., as you might imagine, and have us all laughing to tears.

We learned to strive to be genuine and authentic by the best role model in the world; her "authentic" plastic pearls; her not coloring her hair (by the way, she was beautiful to the day she died); her hugging of an HIV/AIDS patient at a time when his own mother wouldn't do so; her standing by her man with a little rhyming poetry in the 1984 election.

And in a thousand other ways, Barbara Pierce Bush was real and that is why people admired and loved her so.

Finally, our family has had a front seat to the most amazing love story.

Through a multitude of moves: from New Haven

to Odessa to Ventura to Bakersfield to Compton to Midland to Houston to DC to New York to DC to Beijing to DC to Houston to DC and back to Houston and Kennebunkport; their love was the constant in our lives...

The last time my mom went into the hospital, I think Dad got sick on purpose so he could be with her. That's my theory, at least, because literally a day later he showed up with an illness.

He came into her room while she was sleeping and held her hand. His hair was standing straight up, he had on a mask to improve his breathing, and he was wearing a hospital gown. In other words, he looked like hell!

Mom opened her eyes and said, **My God, George, you are devastatingly handsome.**

Every nurse, doctor, staffer had to run to the hallway because they all started crying.

I hope you can see why we think our mom and our dad are teachers and models for our entire family and for many others.

Finally, the last time I was with her, I asked her about dying. Was she ready to go? Was she sad?

Without missing a beat, she said, **Jeb, I believe in Jesus and he is my savior. I don't want to leave your dad, but I know I will be in a beautiful place.**

Mom, we look forward to being with you and Robin and all of God's children. We love you!

THE REVEREND RUSSELL LEVENSON

Ganny's Garden, given by friends and loved ones of Barbara Pierce Bush, is a lovely spot to rest and reflect near downtown Kennebunkport. There you'll find, on a sculpted bench, a wide-brim sunhat—the kind Barbara wore in her garden—and an open copy, facedown, of her favorite book, Jane Austen's *Pride and Prejudice*.

Jane Austen uses one of her characters in that book to utter a wonderful truth: "I declare after all there is no enjoyment like reading! How much sooner one tires of anything than of a book!" Reading and literacy for all was, as you know, Barbara Bush's great passion.

Every great book has a good beginning—but also an end. It falls to me today to speak about the end of someone whose life reads like the consummate "good read."

You are gathered today in this holy space that has been the worshipping community of President George H. W. Bush and First Lady Barbara Bush for over fifty years. It is a privilege to speak as her pastor, priest, friend, and confidant—but what an interesting thing to be a confidant to a woman who has no secrets. What you saw was what you got—what was "in here" [pointing to head] often came "out here" [pointing to mouth].

The author of our lesson in Proverbs muses on the gifts of a loving wife and mother—a godly woman—all of which Barbara had. She believed in, and practiced, the principles of honesty, tolerance, decency, courage, strength—and humility. She lived what has been the mantra of the Bush family for many years—"Don't get caught up in the big 'me.'" One day while I was with her on the beach in Kennebunkport, a fella came up and said, "Hey, you look a lot like Barbara Bush." Without missing a beat, Barbara just said, **Yes, I hear that a lot.**

She was a friend to people of every political persuasion, race, religion. Her generosity of spirit did not draw lines that kept others out; hers was a life of circles that sought to bring others in. Here in Houston, you would see her at every major gala, behind home plate at the Astros games, praying here in the pews, catching up with a neighbor while pushing her own buggy through Walgreens.

One day after sharing prayers and Communion with the president and Barbara, my wife leaned over to kiss the president on the cheek, at which point, Bibi, one of her beloved dogs, nipped her on the calf. Apologies came; but the next morning, on our doorstep was a beautiful orchid with a handwritten note. **Dear Laura, I am so sorry about the bite, you just looked good enough to eat.**

Oh my word, we could all talk endlessly could we not about how great this woman is, but then we are reminded in the lesson from Ecclesiastes that there comes a time for everything—even the end of a great story.

The least of Barbara's virtues was patience. If you were sharing a meal, or waiting on her favorite drink (bourbon and water, for the record), and things were slowing up, she would ask, **Why the holdup?** Barbara liked to see things move along—and I think that is why we are here today.

I think Barbara was becoming impatient. She was tired of waiting on that next chapter. So, well, she welcomed it this past Tuesday—but perhaps this will help those of us she left behind.

Jesus was her pathway to God. She honored and believed that others found God in their own way, but for her—being a Christian mattered. We were talking one day when she looked me in the eye and said, **I am a Christian. I do believe. I want to be confirmed.** She asked if she had to take a class—and I told her, I thought she could teach one (she taught Sunday school here for many years). So, in May of 2015, she and some family gathered in our chapel and she confirmed her faith in Christ; not something she wore on her shoulder—just something very personal, but very real.

She confirmed simply what we believe in this place, what we heard, in the lesson from Second Corinthians, that we live not by what we see, but by faith—things we don't see. So, as Paul writes, even on days like today, we don't lose heart. Yes, Barbara's health declined, but as we just heard, "Though our outer nature is wasting away, our inner nature is being renewed every day...for what is mortal," Paul writes, by the grace and mercy of God, is "swallowed up by life."

We find Barbara's Jesus in the Gospel lesson—a Jesus who says, all that come to Me will be welcomed...the kind who offers the hope that life here, when it comes to its natural close, is changed, not ended.

Some good books have not an ending, but a teaser on what the sequel will look like. Can we imagine this day? A reunion with her parents; with your parents, sir; with your dear Robin. My guess is she has already hunted down Jane Austen and has said, "Well, how did things turn out with Mr. Darcy and Elizabeth Bennet?"

In the meantime, until our time comes, she would want us to carry on, to live as she lived—fully, deeply;

to laugh—often; to love all God sends our way; and to serve one another, the common good, the purposes of God.

So leave here today, not in grief. We will sing as we leave—by Barbara's choice—"Joyful, joyful, we adore Thee." Barbara would want us to celebrate her great next chapter. Barbara Bush has been raised to new life, for in this story, you never turn the page and see the two words *the end*. For Barbara's story has just begun again—and the best is yet to come! Amen.

EPILOGUE

So, if you have read every word of this book, you now know what Barbara Bush's children have known since our birth:

Sit up straight; say "please" and "thank you"; tell the truth; think of others.

Don't buy what you can't afford; return dinner invitations; don't ever put in the last puzzle piece if it's not your puzzle.

Read. Read especially to your children. Read for pleasure. Read to learn. Read to expand your world.

Faith, family, and friends are the only things you really need in life.

And you know that Barbara Bush was undoubtedly one of the most interesting, fascinating, and, yes, bossy women who walked among us. How blessed was I to be her daughter?

This book was written not only to share the joy that was Barbara Bush, but also to help advance her life's work and passion: to make America a more literate country. All the author's proceeds from *Pearls of Wisdom* are being donated to the Barbara Bush Foundation for Family Literacy and will be used to promote the programs and research that will see Mom's dream realized.

Thank you so much for taking this journey down memory lane with us. We appreciate your interest in Mom and your support for literacy.

And don't forget what Mom used to say: **You have two choices in life. You can choose to like your life and be happy; or not like your life and be grumpy. Choose "happy."**

Doro Bush Koch
Daughter of Barbara Bush
Honorary chair
Barbara Bush Foundation for Family Literacy

About the Author

Barbara Bush was born on June 8, 1925, in Rye, New York, to Marvin and Pauline Pierce. She died on April 17, 2018, in Houston, Texas.

But you already know all this. You know that faith, family, and friends were most important to her. You know she was a loyal friend. You know she was a champion of literacy. You know she didn't like people who put in the last puzzle piece.

Here are some things maybe you didn't know about Barbara Pierce Bush:

- Mrs. Bush always swore George Bush was the only boy she ever kissed. They met at a Christmas dance in December 1941 when she was sixteen and he was seventeen. President Bush asked a mutual friend to introduce them, he asked her to dance, and they were together for the next seventy-three years.
- During the war, young Barbara Bush was part

of the "Rosie the Riveter" generation of women as she worked for a brief period in a nuts and bolts factory.

- She started keeping a diary in 1948 and faithfully made entries almost until the day she died.

- She learned to needlepoint in 1962 when President Bush was running for chairman of the Republican Party of Harris County, Texas. She attended all the precinct meetings with him and feared she might fall asleep while hearing his stump speech for the hundredth time. So she began to needlepoint during the events and she never stopped.

- She loved peppermint ice cream.

- Jane Austen was her favorite author, and *Pride and Prejudice* was her favorite book.

- President Bush called her the "Silver Fox."

- When she left the White House, she decided to give up her Secret Service protection and started driving again for the first time in twelve years (eight years as wife of the vice president and four years as First Lady). Her husband bought her a station wagon for Houston, and a convertible for Maine; she could never see out of the windows, so he replaced it with a Smart car. Her driving skills were, well, interesting. After 9/11, her oldest son, then president of the United States, told his mother he was reinstating her Secret Service detail and her driving days were over.

- She hated to cook and was admittedly a bad cook. No one ever disagreed with her on this point.
- She was madly in love with George Herbert Walker Bush until the day she died, holding his hand.